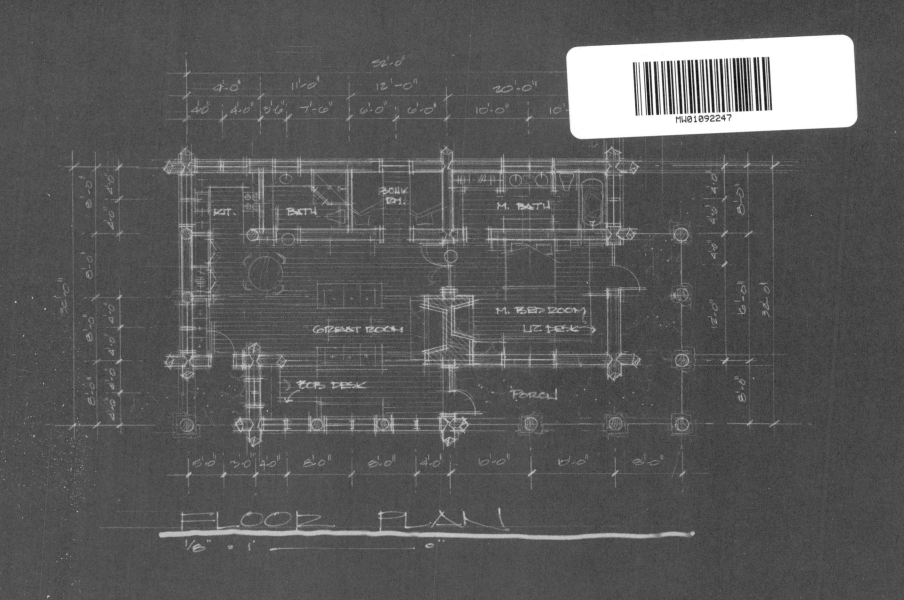

FLOOR PLAN
1/8" = 1'   0"

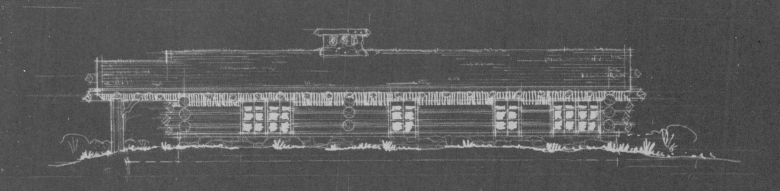

ON

SOUTH ELEVATION
1/8" = 1'   0"

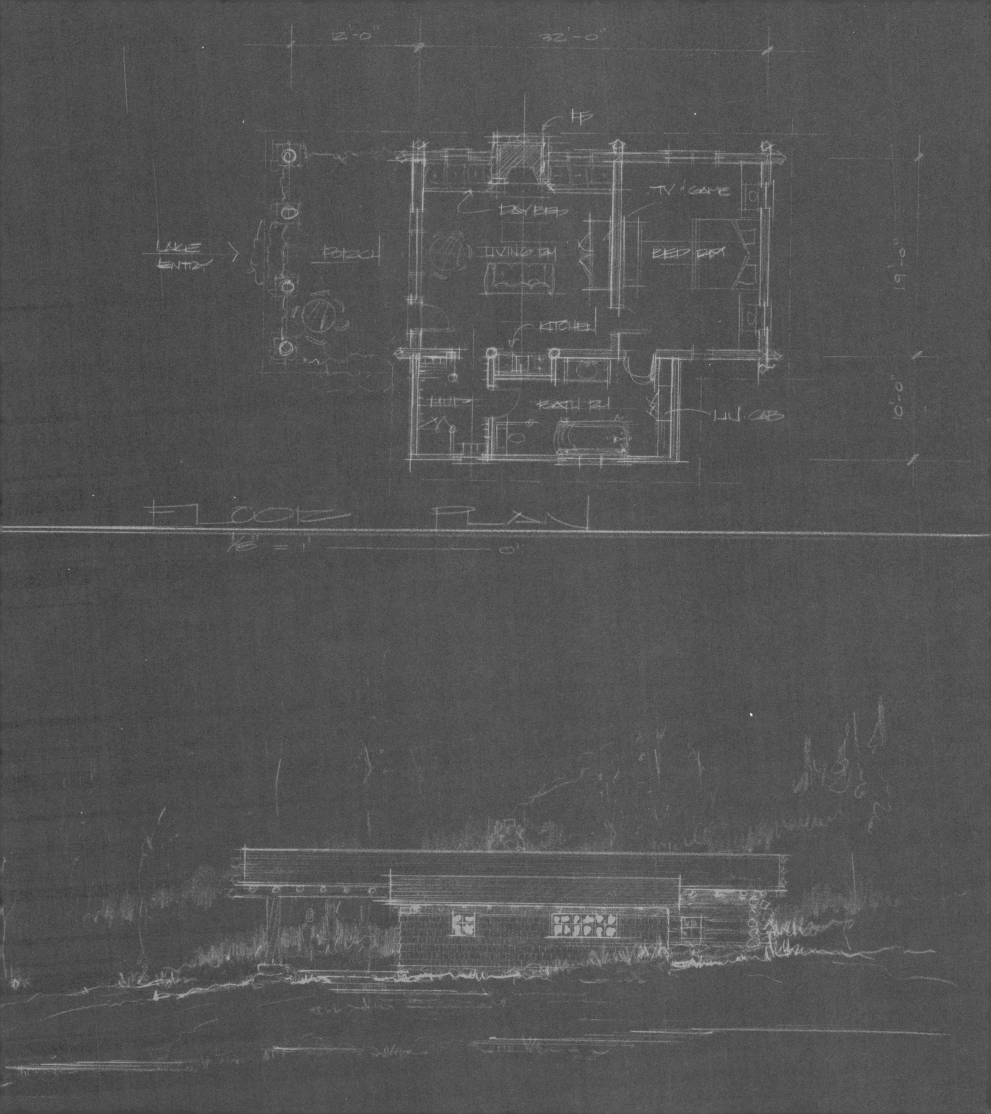

2'-0"   32'-0"

LAKE
ENTRY >

PORCH

DAY BED

LIVING RM

TV & GAME

BED RM

KITCHEN

HUT

BATH RM

LIN · CAB

FLOOR PLAN
1/8" = 1'-0"

19'-0"

10'-0"

The Rustic Cabin

The Rustic Cabin

Design & Architecture

Written & Photographed by

Ralph Kylloe

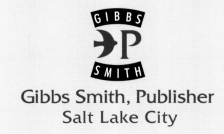

Gibbs Smith, Publisher
Salt Lake City

For my mother,

Elizabeth Ann
1920–2003

Published by
Gibbs Smith, Publisher
P.O. Box 667
Layton, Utah 84041

Orders: 1.800.748.5439
www.gibbs-smith.com

Designed by Kurt Wahlner
Printed in Hong Kong

Library of Congress Cataloging-in-Publication Data

Kylloe, Ralph R.
    The rustic cabin : design & architecture / written and photographed by Ralph Kylloe.—1st ed.
        p. cm.
    ISBN 1-58685-311-2
    1. Log cabins—United States. 2. Log cabins—Decoration—United States. 3. Ranches—United States. I. Title.
NA8470.K95 2003
728.7'3'0973--dc21

2003010847

Contents

Acknowledgments

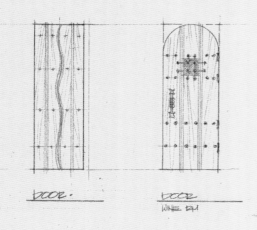

DOOR.   DOOR
        WHITE RM

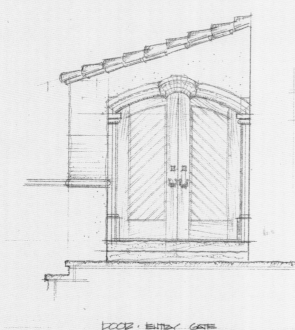

DOOR · ENTRY GATE

I WANTED to call this book *Harry and Larry's Excellent Houses*. But no one would listen to me. My editor, Madge Baird, thought it was a funny title but too unprofessional and frivolous for the title of a big, serious, expensive picture book about architecture. Fully aware that my publishers would not allow me to call it that I struggled for a long time on what exactly I should title this book. Usually I give a manuscript a title when I'm writing the book proposal or outline and then usually wind up changing it as the book progresses. But in truth I still like the title *Harry and Larry's Excellent Houses*. I like it because it accurately depicts the contents of the book. It's trendy and catchy. It's self-explanatory. There is, in reality, nothing to read between the lines. It's honest and people know immediately what the book is all about. It's that simple really. Harry and Larry are, in fact, doing the most advanced, the most extraordinary rustic homes in the world today. I love their stuff! What else is there to say? So there it is!

I always forget to mention someone's name when I say Thank You in the beginning of my books. After the book comes out I usually get a nasty letter from someone or someone says something to me in a bar about my failure to acknowledge someone who helped complete the book. So to avoid this unpleasant confrontation I'm just going to say a very special thanks to everyone in the world, living or dead!

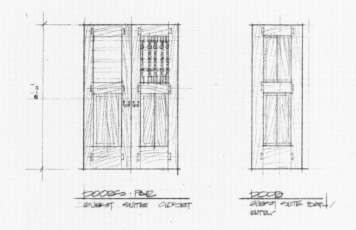

DOORS · PAIR
GUEST SUITE CLOSET

DOOR
GUEST SUITE BATH /
ENTRY

DOOR ·
GARAGE / ENTRY

DOOR
DINING RM

DOOR ·
POWDER RM

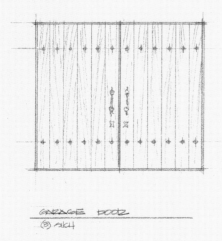

GARAGE DOOR
(3) SKH

I'm serious . . . Thank you all! And I really mean it. This book could not have been completed without your help and I profoundly thank all of you for your contribution. So there!

On the other hand I tried my best to mention all the names of individuals who partook in the construction of the many homes pictured within. But, alas, I am also certain that a thing or two may be mislabeled or I may have incorrectly attributed the creation of something to the wrong individual. In advance, I apologize. Kindly drop me a note and I'll do my best to correct the omission in the next edition.

Apart from that, I will now single out a few souls that kept me on my toes during the entire year that it took for me to complete the writing and make the pictures for this book, including and not limited to the following significant individuals:

Harry Howard and all the wonderful folks at Yellowstone Traditions, Larry Pearson and the creative folks at Larry Pearson Architects including Jacque Spitler and Tashara Pond, the Gaineys, Clyde and Carol Aspevig, Claudia Lee Foster, Brian Kelly, David and Deborah Nice, Bob and Liz Esperti, Fred and Pam Rentschler, Diana Beattie, Greg and Kathy Lemond and family, Dr. and Mrs. Morris, Fran and Frannie Abbott, Pam and Dick Brown, as always, my incredible editor Madge Baird (how she tolerates me I don't know), Gibbs Smith, my brother Kurt Kylloe, and a cast of many. But in truth I can't say thanks enough to my wife Michele and my daughter Lindsey. Michele runs my gallery, takes perfect care of my daughter and never complains when I'm gone too long. Sweetheart, I promise once this book is done I'll help with the dishes!

Introduction

SOMEWHERE in the seven pounds of gray matter that rests between our ears we hear tiny voices. We don't usually know what's being said but we know something is up. Something is not quite right with our lives, the voice seems to be saying. But because most of us are usually tired at the end of the day and because our kids want us to watch another episode of *Sponge Bob* with them and it's our turn to take out the garbage and walk the dog, etc., we struggle to respond correctly to the voices. Don't get me wrong: there is a difference between hearing real voices and longing for something unknown. You don't have to run to your local exorcist just because you feel the need for something in your life that is not quite tangible.

For years now, we've driven our metal vehicles to our condos and houses made of cement and Sheetrock and covered with vinyl siding. We sleep on mattresses made of springs and walk on carpets made of rayon and other kinds of unknown stuff. We wear rubber gloves while we wash our

dishes and then put the semi-clean plates in a machine that washes them for us a second time. We are bombarded with bazillions of electrons as we watch mindless TV programs and eat our processed food on clay and ceramic plates with stainless steel utensils. In the mornings we work out on our exercycles and then have coffee and Pop Tarts for breakfast. At work we sit on phones all day and look at computer screens.

But just for a moment consider this: We were raised in huts and caves and shacks made of stone, sticks and logs. And in these shelters we learned how to communicate with others. Just imagine for a second that we actually spoke with each other for long periods of time. No TVs. No computers. Just talk. Imagine all the stories that were told. Imagine how we laughed together. Imagine how close families became. In truth, maturation is a clear function of social interaction. Just because we are getting older does not mean that we are getting better. We grow because we interact with others. And for millions of generations we learned how to communicate. We practiced it minute by minute. It was in these cabins that we cultivated our humanity. It was there that we became "human." Rustic cabins became forever endeared to us, for it was there that we became what we are today.

Further, the organic nature of logs speaks of freedom. The sensuous curves of logs are erotic in their own right. The long lines of horizontal logs often dazzle us with their mystery and intrigue. The lines remind me of vistas and horizons. Like gazing at the demarcation between sea and air, the lines of logs offer a glimpse of infinity, of the unknown.

At the same time there's humor inherent in log homes.

Big Hole River Ranch, main lodge.

For some reason I often chuckle and smile to myself when I first see a home of logs. Often, dead standing trees that were used in the building of rustic cabins are full of the traces of bark beetles and other insects that left amazing patterns in the logs as they feasted on the wood. I find that following the trails left by such insects leaves me with a sense of awe at the mysteries of nature. The full realization that even tiny insects have full, complete lives that are neither understood nor comprehended by humans instills in me a passionate reverence for life.

Rustic homes offer a sense uncompromising honesty. There is no attempt to hide or disguise the very nature of the material from which they are made. Trees treat us with respect and allow us to live. Somewhere in the back of our minds we know that trees and humans have a symbiotic relationship. They breathe in the carbon dioxide that we exhale. And from CO_2 they graciously create oxygen, which gives us breath. Trees provide us with shelters of all sorts and paper to allow us to record our thoughts. Even when the trees are dead they can provide warmth to keep us comfortable. We are inexorably connected to trees.

SO, THE HUMAN RACE is very old. We've gone through all kinds of changes since we've been here. Truthfully, we're not the most stable creatures on earth, but we try. Some things are constant however: We've always sought shelter. We've always needed to protect ourselves from the elements, from nasty creatures and, occasionally, from ourselves. Although we are dramatically social creatures, we also seek individuality.

Opposite:
Corral Creek Ranch.

Architect's sketch, the Hacienda.

4

Opposite:

Living room, Big Hole River Ranch main lodge.

We want privacy. We want something or some place that is our own. We need to influence our own environment. We seek to express ourselves. We love to collect and decorate things. And all of us acknowledge beauty of some sort.

Like many other emotions, beauty is hard to articulate, for language is incredibly limited. What does a painting or a tune really mean? Who knows? We don't have adequate answers. Why art exists at all is not easily understood. But for most of us, it increases the quality of our lives. Even so, one person loves one thing and someone else thinks it's stupid or ugly. If you like something—great! If you don't, then some will say you have no taste. But what does it matter? Our thoughts and tastes are uniquely our own.

Sometimes, though, art shouts to us and we all hear it at the same time. Greatness is recognized. Originality stands alone. Innovation moves us all. God bless Elvis and Frank Lloyd Wright and the Beatles!

THE BACK-TO-NATURE movement has been espoused by every generation since Socrates stood shouting to us, "Yo, dude! C'mon back." So we did. And for years now people have been traipsing around in the woods, installing wood stoves and antler chandeliers in homes, keeping plants and pets, watching birds, wearing groovy outdoor clothes, fly-fishing, hunting, and building nice modern log homes with all the gadgetry and conveniences that we can afford.

Now that we've done that for years, what's next? Well, that's where "art" comes in.

The Architect

AS A YOUNG GUY, Larry Pearson loved the outdoors. As he matured, he really liked pottery and ceramics. It was the act of sculpting that fascinated him. The great pottery (e.g., Grueby, Weller) was influenced by fruits and vegetables, you know . . . natural stuff. Next time you're at the grocery store, pick up a cucumber and really handle it and look at it. Once you do this you'll know immediately where Grueby pottery came from. Larry also loved photography.

In time, Larry went to the University of Santa Cruz and majored in environmental design with a minor in environmental architecture. His hero was the European design wizard Le Corbusier. He also loved the California Arts and Crafts movement and the extraordinary works of the Greene and Greene brothers. He was both inspired and influenced by Japanese architecture and by the 1930s efforts of California architect Bernard Maybeck. He traveled extensively in Europe, marveling at the many different styles of design.

After working in historic preservation in California for a while, he found his way to Montana, where he worked developing a huge private compound somewhere in the woods. He won't say for whom it was built or where it was. The project took two years. He fell in love with the historic regional structures of Montana and eventually opened an office in Big Fork. Later he went on to Bozeman, where his home and practice are today. He goes by the name of Larry Pearson Architects, AIA. He surrounds himself with competent people, including the queen of all office directors, Jacque Spitler. So far, he's done

Rock, log and landscape
work at Corral Creek Ranch.

R i g h t :

**Attic bedroom, Double D
Ranch.**

about a hundred structures. Barns, homes, fire towers, cabins, and pavilions of all sizes are his "thing." All of them are extraordinary. He is a brilliant mover and shaker of the rustic design business.

The Style

"PARKITECTURE" is a recent addition to the often-misunderstood nomenclature of architects, designers and park historians. Beginning in the early 1900s and lasting well into the 1930s, designers were commissioned to create a style of architecture that would be appropriate for the country's blossoming love affair with the newly established National Park System. Many of the early architects were strongly influenced

9

Opposite:

Entryway, Fir Creek Ranch.
Table by David Laitman, chairs
made of Indiana hickory.

by the classic European and Scandinavian-chalet styles. The Prairie School style of Frank Lloyd Wright and the Arts and Crafts movement engendered by Gustav Stickley also influenced parkitecture efforts.

The driving force of the movement was, nonetheless, rebellion from the excessively ornate embellishments of the Victorian period. Americans sought simplicity in design; they wanted something natural, something that would withstand the test of time. Consequently, the great structures of the national parks were created with indigenous timber and stone, harvested and dug from the immediate surroundings.

And, so, many of the homes being designed and constructed today have their roots in the great halls of lodges in such national treasures as Yellowstone, Glacier, Yosemite, Bryce Canyon, Mt. Hood, the Grand Canyon, and Mt. Rainier. Anyone who has the opportunity to spend some time in these buildings becomes fully aware of their historic significance. There is little wonder as to their influence on today's regional rustic architectural trends.

Although new, the articulation of the Regional Rustic style of design is critical to its continuing evolution. Regional Rustic design is, in reality, part folk art, part the inspiration of nature, and part guided by the technical aspects and dictates of engineering and technology—but you wouldn't know it by looking at it. Almost all of the structures within this realm look old, feel old, smell old and are, for the most part, old. But in truth they're brand new. Just the visible materials are old.

The buildings are part of the environment, part of the landscape. Organic architecture, as Larry sometimes refers to

A stone dining set is the
site of lunches and
evening cocktails at the
Hacienda.

it, utilizes indigenous materials. The forms inherent on the site influence the very nature of the buildings. The forms of the structures and the buildings seem to grow from the ground. The colors inherent in this form of design are natural. The colors utilized blend with the environment. Look outside your window and see what's there: those are the colors you want to incorporate.

Further, the Regional Rustic genre encourages the integration of the earth and water into the architecture. The landscape dictates the type of building to be built. Restructuring the land only minimally is critical. Trees, as much as possible, are left untouched. You won't see bulldozers chopping up the land. Boulders and streams are gifts from the heavens.

There has to be a controlled relationship between nature and the buildings. Views are important, as is the inherent dignity of the land. Great architecture is about enjoying nature. Regional Rustic design is about the relationship of the landscape to the structure. They must work in harmony. The genre believes in an inspirational approach to design rather than a strict, structured, academic servitude to architecture and engineering dogmas. Good design focuses on passion, on feelings. Homes should not be museums where one can look but not touch. One should absolutely be able to put one's feet up on the coffee table. Walk around barefoot. Toss another log on the fire. Have some friends over. Talk to each other. Pet the dog. Relax.

Good architecture allows for a continuum of experiences. Light should dance around the room. Organic design allows the experience of a room to change as the day grows older and as the new day begins. Flow and balance are critical. Homes should have movement. They need to have soul.

Log homes designed in an organic nature, however, have a profound feel to them. When dead standing trees are used we feel a kinship with them. Their knots and twists and curves dance with movement. Their inherent rich hues speak deeply to us. The traces on old logs, left by bark beetles and other insects, remind us of the very nature from where we come. The moss on the rocks begs us to touch. Flat-stacked stones look the way nature intended them to be. Chimneys and porch pillars should look like they're growing from the ground. They should look like trees and mountains.

Harry Meets Larry

HARRY HOWARD is a painter; actually he's an artist. He does landscapes—watercolors, oils and other mediums. He's very good at it. He graduated with a degree in fine arts in 1976 from Washington State University and made his living for many years as a landscape painter.

Dennis Derham started Yellowstone Log Restorations around 1985. He was the driving force for many years with the company. Shortly, Harry Howard bought into the company. Initially they restored structures. In 1988 they became Yellowstone Traditions, based in Bozeman, Montana.

Harry Howard and Larry Pearson met, by chance, on a project in Jackson Hole, Wyoming. They got along and a few years later Larry joined Yellowstone Traditions (YT) as a staff

The barn at Corral Creek Ranch houses horses on the main floor and hay and other ranch necessities above. Dead standing lodgepole pine is the primary building material.

architect. A few years later Larry wandered off to open his own business.

Around 1994, Harry was invited to build a house on a vast tract of land just off the Madison River in Montana. Rather than construct a trophy house just to expose the owners to exactly what a great Montana residence can look like, they constructed a small "line cabin" high up on the owners' property, just below the tree line. Harry lived on-site for six months and home-schooled his kids there. All the materials for the cabin were harvested from the immediate grounds. The result was an absolutely charming, small cabin full of character and ambiance. (See Corral Creek in this book.) The owners loved it! And they proceeded over the next several years to have Larry and YT design and build many of the structures that are presently on the property.

Harry and Larry are a couple of crazy guys. I love both of them. They are nonstop balls of energy, bursting with enthusiasm. They have the ability to get excited about their projects. Their understanding and comprehension of beauty is profoundly infectious. They are masters at their jobs. They love what they do. They are the chief innovators and proponents of the genre of Regional Rustic design.

Yellowstone Traditions Philosophy

AT YT, their approach and philosophy is consistent with the genre of Regional Rustic design as described above. They focus on the soul of the environment. The landscape comes first. They love to utilize recycled materials and reclaim abused and misused land. Homes, they say, are portraits on a landscape.

Harry Howard describes YT as a group of artisans masquerading as contractors. They never advertise. Word-of-mouth brings them a variety of eager clients. Their concept is that they do not build houses; rather, they engage in an artistic endeavor to increase the quality of life of the owners as well as the individual artisans. They foster creativity. They encourage problem solving and they build relationships. They empower individuals. Workers walk away from their projects each day feeling good about themselves. And frankly, they are extraordinary at what they do.

Not only does YT build all kinds of rustic structures, it also has a complete in-house custom-design workshop run by rustic artist Todd Gardener. Todd builds many of the windows and doors, as well as intricate cabinets and furnishings of all types, that are used in the projects.

The clients that come to Harry and Larry are sophisticated. They are opinionated and talented. They have discriminating taste and know what they want. They seek quality and originality. They know how to motivate people. They want the best.

The homes showcased in this book are the result of a profound collaboration between owners, architect and builders. There is an astonishing temptation to look at a house as a sterile entity. In reality, thousands of decisions have to be made along the way. Houses have lives of their own. They reflect a passionate interaction that is clearly an artistic effort.

Art is a good thing. It helps us to become better people. Not only can our homes reflect the guiding principles of art but we can also lead our own lives in the spirit of quality and uniqueness. It's okay to be good at something. It's okay to have a really wonderful house. It's okay to strive for uniqueness and originality. That's how it should be.

Hickory chairs enhance the ambiance of Corral Creek Ranch.

Moose Meadows Ranch

The entryway to the home further reveals the dramatic lines often inherent in log cabins.

O p p o s i t e :

Created with applied ancient timbers, the home offers four bedrooms and a comfortable living room complete with contemporary furnishings.

O v e r l e a f :

(Left) With a driveway that seems to go on for miles, the Moose Meadow Ranch was designed by architect Larry Pearson. When driving to the home, one must slow down to avoid hitting any number of elk that wander into the front yard.

(Right) A delightful driftwood chandelier blends perfectly with the timbers and ancient wood used in construction of the home.

A FEW DAYS BEFORE my visit, it had been thirty below zero and the snow crunched when I walked on it; miles away, I had noticed a tiny speck on the side of a frozen mountain. Today there was four feet of snow on the ground and I was happy to be in a four-wheel-drive vehicle. Earlier in the day, a bulldozer had removed mountains of snow from the driveway. Without it, there would have been be no way I could get to the house.

Completed in the fall of 2003, the home was designed by Larry Pearson. The site of the home included twenty-four acres, but the view from just about anyplace inside went on for miles, and included stunning panoramas of the Bridger Range and Paradise Valley. William Keshishian of Elephant Builders in Gallatin Gateway, Montana, completed the home in thirteen months. From the beginning, although it was to be a 4,100-square-foot home, it was determined that it was to be a cost-efficient project. The owners, who had wandered Montana for years with dreams of having a second home in the area, wanted a building that could be an effective family compound.

The home includes numerous built-in bookcases, as well as a large entertainment center that hides the family's TV and other electronic devices.

Opposite:

A view from the upstairs balcony shows the massive floor-to-ceiling fireplace and the well-appointed living room.

A stick-built frame helped keep the costs under control, and solid sprayed-foam insulation makes the house airtight. It has four bedrooms, a massive fireplace created by stonemason Jeff Madson, a study and a game room that includes a pool table overlooking the living room. The exterior includes extensive porches and an outside stone fireplace with a grill for cooking and entertaining. In the kitchen are granite tops on counter spaces and an efficient stainless steel refrigerator. The dining room table was made from the base of a huge lodgepole pine that was found submerged on the bottom of Flat Head Lake.

Because of the proximity to valleys and mountains, the snow loads in the immediate region are often massive, so the roof of the home was engineered to tolerate heavy weight. Designed with true log construction, it was covered with steel to allow for the quick melting of snow.

The floors were covered with antique pine boards that were milled for tongue-and-groove construction. Hickory chairs for the dining room and hickory bar stools for the kitchen counter area complete the ambience.

The home is a wonder of efficiency. The owners can relax in front of a large-screen TV housed in an entertainment center, or simply enjoy the afternoons watching the herds of elk and deer wander past their door!

The kitchen recesses off the living room by a bar that serves as a counter for quick meals. Hickory chairs serve as dining room chairs at the bar and around the dining table.

Left:

Built-in pine cabinets house dishes and stainless steel appliances allow the owners to cook hot meals on cold winter nights.

The kitchen island was fashioned from an old carpenter's bench.

Opposite:

Icicles hang down from the roof and blend with the old-world timbers used to construct the home.

The bath off the master bedroom includes a tiled walk-in shower big enough for two.

If you don't like showers, then this large bathtub with numerous jets is also big enough for two! The low windows allow you to watch out for any moose that may be eyeing the running water!

Double D Ranch

Out the front door lies this small pavilion that includes a fire pit, table and chairs. The majestic Gallatin River flows a few thousand feet directly below the patio.

The interior of the home is complete with a corner fireplace with a western-motif fire screen, a center beam that seems to always have been there and rafters made from old timbers.

Overleaf:

Designed by architect Larry Pearson, this twelve-hundred-square-foot home is a model of simplicity, and comfort.

*I*F YOU SUFFER FROM VERTIGO or don't like heights or rattlesnakes, go somewhere else. If you want the thrill of unprecedented mountain views along with the hominess and comfort of a small, intimate rustic cabin, then this is your kind of place.

Designed as a guest cabin by architect Larry Pearson and built by On Site Management, Inc., of Bozeman, Montana, this structure resides comfortably on a remote section of a huge cliff. It is definitely high-drama property and construction of the building was not without its difficulties. Materials had to be transported over a small, unsteady bridge that was built in the 1920s. Because the owners wanted a secluded cabin, the power lines for the building were placed underground. The twelve-hundred-square-foot building was completed with true log construction as the center core. Conventionally built add-ons were attached to the core. The pumped septic system was added on a sloped site.

Greg Olmstead Masons used stones collected on the property for the fireplace and surround. A patio with a breathtaking view complete with grill, table and chairs allows one to have a bird's-eye view of eagles fishing on the river directly below the home!

The cabin was intended to be approached on foot, and Mayville Landscaping of Bozeman, Montana, tied the house back to the hill with native stones and restored the land by planting indigenous sagebrush and other grasses. An old

Once the home was complete, landscapers restored the grounds by planting indigenous flora around the home.

The bath contains a built-in sink outlined with ornate, western-influenced tiles. A claw-foot tub and attached shower allows one to "freshen up" after a hard day of "kickin' the brush!"

The dining area contains this ornate continental sideboard and upholstered side chairs.

The kitchen is complete with slate-top counters and this burgundy Elmira stove.

game trail serves as a path to the building.

The home was tastefully appointed with regional and traditional "goodies." The kitchen includes a gorgeous burgundy Elmira stove. The counters are topped with slate. The living room is complete with rich leather chairs, while the corner fireplace is adorned with a pictorial fire screen. The center of the home includes a structural beam organically molded into the large rock found on the property and now located in the center of the living room.

A small bunk room off the rear of the building has organic posts and tasteful bed covers. A very small upstairs loft (that requires one to maneuver on one's knees) offers built-ins and beds made of antique barn boards. A small dining area is not only comfortable with upholstered side chairs but made functional with a continental sideboard and mirror as well.

The bathroom contains a contoured claw-foot tub with attached showerhead and curtain. The master bedroom contains an impressive bed with western motif resting on lush burgundy carpets. Tasteful decorative items of all sorts are placed throughout the home.

But there is more than just logs and furniture to this house. It is a receptacle of pragmatic folklore. Although rattlesnakes used to frequent the house, since the owner surrounded the home with a single coil of hemp rope, as advised by ancient cowboy lore, not a single snake has been seen! Our hats are off to the wisdom of the cowboys and to those who follow their sage advice.

A b o v e :

A back bedroom contains this highly organic bunk bed. Small in size, the home comfortably sleeps ten.

L e f t :

Tucked underneath the rafters, the owners often enjoy quiet meals around the small dining table.

The loft includes two built-in beds. One must
ascend a small ladder and travel on one's knees
to get to the beds.

Reminiscent of the old hotels of the west, a "cushy" leather sofa sits in the living room.

The corner fireplace not only looks great, but also provides enough heat to take the chill off cold winter nights.

O p p o s i t e :

The master bed's tall headboard is adorned with an Indian chief carving. A plush leather ottoman sits at the footboard and provides a place to put your boots on as the sun comes up in the east.

Fishtail Basin

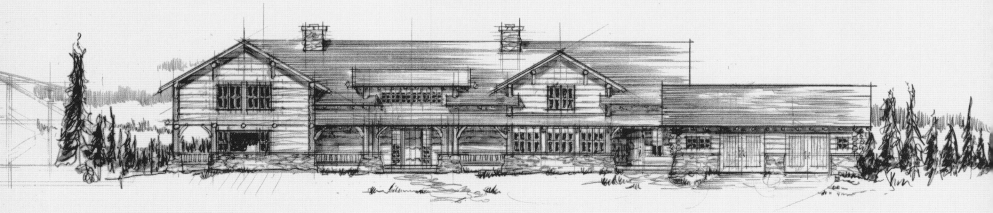

The front entrance to the home shows dormers and pillars designed in the classic Arts and Crafts style.

*T*RAVELING DOWN a long, winding road in the middle of nowhere, I came across a small restaurant named Grizzly. Since I needed directions, I parked and went in. "Turn right down the road a piece," was all the bartender said. I drove down the road and turned right. I pulled into a ranch setting and was chased by several farm dogs. After the dogs settled down, the geese had their way with me. There is no rest for the weary.

It was a complete working ranch but no one was around. "This must be it," I thought to myself. I took out my cameras and started taking pictures. And I must say that I was, from the start, disappointed. This was clearly not a designer home. But I was here and would do my job to the best of my ability. This was a ranch with old buildings, old tractors, chickens, dogs, horses, goats, geese and cows. It looked like a farm and smelled like a farm and wasn't at all what I expected. After an hour of making photos, I asked one of the hands if I could go inside to make more. "No problem," he said, as chewing tobacco ran down his chin. An hour later, someone asked what I was doing. He broke into hysterics and told me that I was at the wrong farm. I felt like an idiot. I packed up and started to drive away when the hand told me that

Complete with stonework, old logs, dormers and overhangs, Fishtail
Basin sits just across the northern rim of Yellowstone National Park.

Previous overleaf:

(Left) A small family dining room
is complete with western-influenced chairs and a roaring fireplace. The red painted cabinet
offers energy to the setting.

(Right) A large balcony sits off the master bedroom and allows the owners to
watch the roving herds of elk wander by.
A satellite dish is unobtrusively placed
on the backside of the home.

The drama of the home is easily evident from the second-floor balcony. The chandeliers are classic western motif. The home is heated through the square stones in the floor. (Left) Striped fabric and leather upholstery are comfortable companions with the massive stone fireplace on the opposite end of the home.

the ranch I wanted was just a bit far-ther down the road.

First, I drove through a thick growth of aspen trees, next along rolling hills of high-desert vegetation, and then into a thick growth of pon-derosa trees. This road, like many in the Montana wilderness, was nothing more than two ruts for tires and dust. Groundhogs laughed at me as I navi-gated the trail.

Then, on the horizon arose the mighty Bear Tooth Mountains that outline the northern rim of Yellowstone National Park. I stopped the car and in the background I could hear an engine running. "I must be close," I thought. I drove on and moments later appeared a structure that, like many of the other homes I had visited, seemed to be a complete extension of the landscape. Large in size, the home blended perfectly with the surroundings. It appeared to grow directly from the ground.

After driving up the entrance-

Another view of the northern fireplace shows built-in cabinets and a variety of decorative items.

This built-in cabinet was made of rough-cut pine boards in the cabinet shop at Yellowstone Traditions. A small game table with antique hickory chairs is the site of chess matches, checkers and card games on cool evenings and rainy days.

The kitchen is complete with copper countertops, built-in ranges and uphol-stered hickory bar stools.

way, I got out of my car and knocked on the door. No one answered. I knocked louder. No one was home. In time, I just opened the door and went in. I probably shouldn't have done that, but once inside, I felt like I had gone to heaven. I hoped (really hard) that I was in the right place—I had to be! Full of passionate colors and vibrating with the horizontal and vertical designs of logs, I was swept away with the beauty of the place. I just stood there, taking it all in. After almost an hour, caretakers Amanda Hansen and Jami Mendy wandered in. They were so casual that I immediately felt welcome. I introduced myself and found out that I was there a day early! Nonetheless, I was invited in and given the grand tour.

The owners had chosen the site and played a significant role in the evolution of the building. Wanting a large, central great hall for their family of five boys and many friends, they articulated their ideas to architect Larry Pearson. The owners were a close family who not only partook in indoor family activities but also enjoyed riding their many horses and hiking in the spectacular setting.

Pearson made the initial drawings on a napkin in the presence of the owners. Eventually, bedrooms, kitchens, fireplaces and porches were added to the design. Master color artist Jennifer Besson was hired to customize colors for the many rooms in the home. The interior design firm of Kibler and Kitch of Red Lodge, Montana, was brought in for furnishings and advice on décor.

The entire project was a close family affair. The owners

A pair of single beds in a second-floor bedroom provides resting space for the many visitors to the ranch.

One of the kids' rooms is complete with bunk beds cut from local dead standing trees. Colorful textiles add life to the room as seen from the hide rug on the floor.

The master bedroom contains this four-poster bed made of local hard wood draped with light fabric.

A highly decorated armchair and footstool, in classic western design, rests in one of the many bedrooms of the home.

A barbecue pit sits just off the back parameter of the patio. Frequently used, the style of the stone construction is called flat stacked.

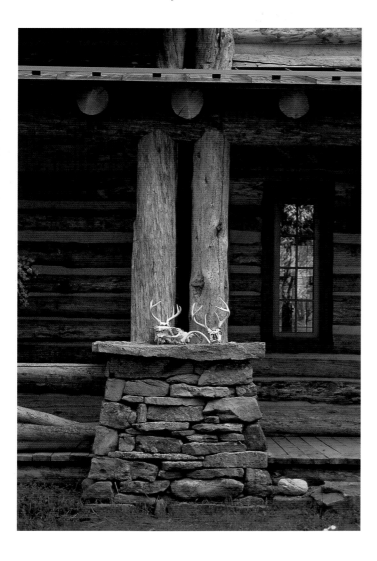

participated directly in all facets of the decision-making process. It took two years to complete the compound. Because of the arid climate and ongoing threat of brush and forest fires, a fire suppression system and metal roof were added to the building. Guy Fairchild of Phil Cox Masonry Co., widely regarded for his stone artistry, was engaged to construct the huge fireplaces and surrounds.

Yellowstone Traditions was the contracting firm and Shaun Ryan oversaw the daily efforts of the crew. The complexity of the entire setting should not be overlooked. Ed Matos of Bridger Engineering (truly the unsung hero of many complicated projects in the Rockies) worked closely with contractors and the architect to solve many of the engineering problems.

From the beginning, great respect was paid to the surrounding environment. The owners are nonhunters and devout conservationists. Ultimately, very few trees were removed for the project. The building was constructed on a concrete slab and heated with innovative in-floor radiant heat. The floor surface was scored and stained to appear as if it were large, interlocking stones. These "stones" were colored to match the native rocks and soil found on the property.

Like many of the homes in the region, the structure was conventionally stick-built, and half-round logs from

Like many of the homes designed in the vernacular of regional rustic design, old logs and stones were used in the construction of the compound. Deer skulls, found on the property, were placed around the home and were set to further the ambiance of the wilderness.

dead standing ponderosa pine trees were applied to both the internal and external surfaces of most of the building. Designed to support unimaginable snow loads, the roof system is constructed with true log rafters and trusses. To maximize efficiency, a sawmill was established on-site.

An overview of the home suggests a warm, intimate setting that reflects the interests and experiences of the family. The sophisticated taste of the owners is evident in the myriad collections and furnishings throughout the home. Much of their time is spent outdoors. Evenings are enchanted, with meals cooked on the outside grill. Moose, bear, elk, deer, coyotes, mountain lions, bobcats, badgers and marmots are ever-present. The mountains behind the home are constantly changing and the colors of nature renew the spirits of anyone who takes the time to ponder the mysteries of life. This home is more than a house or a structure on a piece of property. It's a place where people partake in the great joys of life. It's a place of great art and beauty and is a tribute to the creative spirit of humanity.

A further view of the log and stonework. The outdoor sconces were made of metal and lined with mica.

The rustic nature of the pine-bough sconces blends perfectly with the setting.

The fusion of competent masonry and skilled carpentry can render natural materials into artistic end products. The moss on the rocks adds to the ambiance of the setting.

An antique elk antler armchair, probably made in the Jackson Hole area in the 1930s, sits in the corner next to one of several fireplaces. The colorful Indian blanket and cowboy boots add character to the room.

Big Hole River Ranch

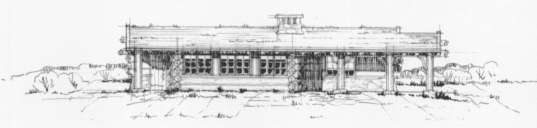

NORTH ELEVATION
1/8" = 1'   0"

EAST ELEVATION
1/8" = 1'   0"

WEST ELEVATION
1/8" = 1'   0"

Front view of one of several small cabins at the Big Hole Ranch. The landscape setting is ideal for fishing and relaxing.

Overleaf:

(Left) An overview of the ranch shows five cabins and the dining lodge. Other buildings also exist on the property for residents and employees. The Big Hole River is seen in the background. The ranch was photographed in the spring when the landscape glowed green. As the seasons mature, browns and yellows of the high-desert plateau dominate the landscape. (Right) The lodge houses an impressive collection of hunting and fishing-related antique items.

*S*OMEWHERE IN THE SOUTHERN PART of Montana flows the Big Hole River. Known as a world-class fishery for monster brown trout, the river flows through mountainous terrain and dry, flat plateaus. Deer, elk and antelope can be seen almost whenever one wants to see them. The wind howls and the cold can kill you. The area is no less gorgeous than it is remote. This land is the stuff of legends, strong spirits, and historical precedents.

A front view of the dining lodge. Low rooflines are typical of many of the historic structures that dot the land.

Big Hole River Ranch lies down winding dirt roads, past cattle ranches that have seen better days and at the edge of vast tracts of wilderness. Occupying two-and-a-half miles of riverfront, the ranch is owned in a partnership by fourteen friends. The compound contains five distinct cabins, a main lodge, and various outbuildings and workers' quarters. It also offers the world's greatest trout-fishing pond, where thirty-inch rainbows (I've caught several of them during my many visits to the camp) will take your toes off if you're not careful.

The owners are able to use the impeccably maintained facility whenever they want. A full-time cook provides all meals in the main lodge, and guests of the owners are always welcome. The main lodge is nothing less then a fly-fisherman's dream. Two built-in fly-tying desks are complete with everything imaginable. If you don't want to tie your own flies, then the shelves are packed with hundreds of different flies. The compound offers the use of any number of drift boats. If you

This stuffed badger watches a roaring fire in the fireplace. Oversized armchairs and bench seating are often occupied in the evening as guests socialize with other members of the club.

Opposite:

A quiet nook in the lodge offers guests the opportunity to read, listen to music, or talk with any number of mounts hanging on the walls.

want a guide, professionals are just a phone call away. Or if you want some serious personal lessons, the managing partner will have you up and casting in no time; he was a member of the U.S. Fly-Fishing Team for years. I have spent many happy hours with him, having the incredibly subtle nuances of fly-fishing knots, techniques and every other aspect of the art drilled into my brain. I can assure everyone that I am a better person and fisherman for it!

When the land for the ranch was first acquired in 1995, a first glance said it was "used" and discarded. Heavily burdened by years of overuse and abuse, the land was reclaimed with great effort. The cattle were removed, as were several buildings.

The founders of the Big Hole River Ranch are discriminating individuals. Their sophisticated taste is evident in everything. They are influential people with the unique ability to put the most common of us (myself included) at complete ease. From the beginning, they insisted on "historical correctness" for the project. Using both indigenous and recycled materials, they sought to blend the camp with the immediate environment. The lodge was built with authentic hand-notch, true log construction.

KIBO Group Architecture designed the initial building. Larry Pearson later added porches and other accent elements. The construction wizards at Yellowstone Traditions

The floors of the lodge were made from rough-cut pine. The dining room table was made from three-inch-thick antique timbers.

A front view of the fireplace in the lodge.

A detail section of the outside wall shows the impressive work of an accomplished mason.

This hand-hewn door was built by the craftsmen at Yellowstone Traditions.

The cabinet holds the fly-fishing vest of Pat Opler, wife of Ed Opler, who was the captain of the U.S. Fly-Fishing Team. The pins were collected over a number of years at international fly-fishing competitions. Her recent death prompted Big Hole Ranch to fly the flag at half-staff.

A further view of the fly-tying room shows the game table and bench seating that offers weary fishermen an opportunity to relax and tell of the day's fish stories.

Opposite:

Arguably the finest fly-tying room in existence. The glass-top table is the home for an extensive collection of antique fly-fishing collectibles. The drawers in the desks are full of flies and more fly-tying gear than you can shake a feather at!

A mountain goat oversees the pool table in the game room.

A bear strikes a threatening pose as it overlooks the pool table.

*For *further photos of Big Hole Ranch, see* Cabins and Camps, *also by Ralph Kylloe.*

were responsible for building the lodge and other "camps" on the grounds. Numerous waterways, including streams, ponds, and in-ground sprinkler systems were created. The result is a place that is nothing less than profound, comfortable, and, if I may say so, absolutely "out of this world."

The interior of the main lodge has oversized, comfortable couches, pool tables, taxidermy of all sorts, isolated nooks for reading, a roaring fireplace, a full-service bar, a gourmet kitchen, and an impressive fly-fishing library—all in a setting reminiscent of the great camps of the past. And, to top it off, they have the largest native brown trout I have ever seen or caught right out their front door!

O p p o s i t e :

An overstuffed chair and reading lamp provide a cozy corner for sampling the impressive collection of adventure reading material housed by the built-in bookcases.

A view of the kitchen demonstrates
how the use of natural materials can
create a profound rustic appeal.

A small island also houses a wet sink in the kitchen. The background wall contains the refrigerator. Rough-cut boards were used to cover the appliances.

Hidden amongst the cabinets are fax machines and electronics of all sorts.

Opposite:

The porches on the building were added by architect Larry Pearson. Using highly figured dead standing materials, the home reflects the local heritage.

The main lodge at the Big Hole Ranch includes a fully stocked bar. Constructed by Yellowstone Traditions, the bar included numerous comfortable western-influenced bar stools.

Juniper Ridge

SOUTH ELEVATION
1/8" = 1'-0"

O v e r l e a f :

(Left) Known as Juniper Ridge, this home was constructed by the creative folks at Yellowstone Traditions. Working in conjunction with the owner, the home was designed by architect Larry Pearson.

(Right) The round chimney was a late add-on that allowed the fireplace to "breathe" and burn more efficiently.

Built to look like it had always been there, the house was completed with a metal roof. As the roof rusts, it blends perfectly with the organic colors found in the area.

WNED BY an internationally known artist and his artist wife, this home is a marvel of simplicity and design. The concept was based on the Scandinavian architecture of his ancestors; he spent significant amounts of time in Norway studying the subtleties and nuances of architecture before he embarked on this project.

Like many of the homes in the Northern Rockies, the setting for Juniper Ridge is in the middle of nowhere. A quart of ice cream is an hour away. But deer and elk graze in the front yard. Bears wander past the house and great fly-fishing is just a few steps from the house.

The owners made a decision early on to blend their home and yard into the existing landscape through riparian management. Next to the house is a small amount of lawn that allows for a tidy yard and attractive flower plantings. The lawn transitions into taller grasses that soon blend into the natural flora of the area. A long-term effort is underway to restore healthy natural plants to the surrounding acreage and replenish the habitat for wild animals.

When this couple was ready to start their new home, they approached Harry Howard of Yellowstone Traditions to build an art studio first. As fate would have it, Harry had

The low overhangs and rust color of the roof lend themselves to the historical character of the area.

A skilled mason and an accomplished carpenter can complement each other. Ancient timbers and local rocks and stones often complement each other in colors.

been a lifelong admirer of the husband's art. Needless to say, they had a lot in common. Architect Larry Pearson was engaged to design a large studio with an attached living space for the couple.

Historical antecedents determined the evolution of the compound. Pearson wanted the structures to be consistent with the architectural history of the valley. They also needed to have a Scandinavian influence as requested by the owner. In

The symmetrical forms integral in the home add to its uniqueness.

truth, the studio was modeled after a chicken coop that Pearson stumbled on one day. Looking more like a barn, the slopping lines and significant overhangs meld the structure to the immediate landscape.

Once the studio was complete, plans were drawn for the main house. For a wood supply, an old barn was located in Twin Bridges, Montana, dissembled and shipped to the new site. The logs were milled on-site and utilized in the construction of the building. Neil Greathouse acted as the superintendent of construction.

Like many clients that have worked with Pearson and YT, the owners were actively involved in both the design and construction process. The husband-and-wife, both accomplished artists, had a deep vision for the home and supported the efforts of the builders and designer in their quest for originality, simplicity, uniqueness and handcrafted quality.

Recycled timbers were applied to the exterior of the stick-built house, blending this new home with historical buildings in the area. Rusted corrugated metal was used on the roof. Bold, handmade metal strap hinges were created by Bill Moore of Red Lodge, Montana, and used on doors and other areas as needed. Original cutout designs were incorporated into both the interior and exterior staircases.

The house is a model of integrated styles of furniture and art. Reproduction Arts and Crafts furniture, simple in design, stabilizes the living/dining room. Colorful antique

Handmade doors by Yellowstone Traditions hang throughout the house. Heavy, handmade strap hinges add a sense of strength to the home.

A dramatic landscape by Clyde Aspevig hangs off the wall. The simple forms of Arts and Crafts furniture blend perfectly with the home.

In honor of the owner's ancestry, Scandinavian motifs and methods were employed in the stair railing. European and Scandinavian antiques, such as Biedermeier, will one day replace the Arts and Crafts furniture.

pieces from Scandinavia are dispersed throughout the home. The owners determined the colors for all the rooms, and even worked trial-and-error with a plaster expert to arrive at the perfect "butter cream" color for the plaster that coats the walls.

Kitchen cabinets were created from ancient, rough-cut timbers; a combination of wood and granite slate was used for the countertops.

The floor in the living room is covered with
bricks. A reproduction Arts and Crafts dining set
complements the setting. A small rectangular
fireplace offers warmth on cool mountain nights.

The symmetry of lines and colors adds to the calmness of the home. The "roundels," the small, round sections of glass at the tops of the windows, were common in historical homes.

A contemporary, even arm settle of Arts and Crafts design allows for a relaxing evening in front of the fireplace. The view out the windows allows the owners to watch the deer and bears feed on the local vegetation.

The Scandinavian influence is evident in the blue-painted cupboard and the cut-outs on the wall shelf.

A soft spotlight down a hallway accentuates framed artwork. Much of the interior of the house was painted in soft yellows to match the colors of the sun.

A further view of the kitchen with both wood and stone countertops. Copper pots and pans blend perfectly with the yellow
painted walls and the hues of antique barn boards.

The design for this artist's studio and attached living quarters came from a historical chicken coop found in the area. The large picture window faces north, allowing for "cool" light to illuminate the studio.

The kitchen is completed with the inclusion of a variety of antique collectibles. The cabinets were made from rough-cut antique boards.

The interior of the artist's studio
has in-floor radiant heat, tract
lighting and massive windows.
When the artist tires of painting,
he often entertains himself by play-
ing the grand piano.

A side view of the artist's studio at
Juniper Ridge demonstrates how lines
of a structure can complement each
other, thus creating a dramatic setting.

Old timbers were utilized on the exposed portions of the home. The cut-outs on the porch are Scandinavian in design.

The home itself is an integrated series of simple yet sophisticated designs. Each small design element, (e.g., the dramatic overhangs on the porches and sunroom, the circular chimney pipe and stone chimney base, the dramatic pillars, etc.) although unique and complete in its own right, fuses with the whole to create a bold sum. Frankly, the building is alive. It has movement and even a touch of humor.

The ancient textures of the building, including the rusted metal roof and the patinated color of the beams and stones, blend to make a statement that language is incapable of conveying. It is a house that transcends time. The home is an absolute landmark of character, art at its finest, in a setting that brings forth indescribable emotions in the viewer.

Two Moose Ranch

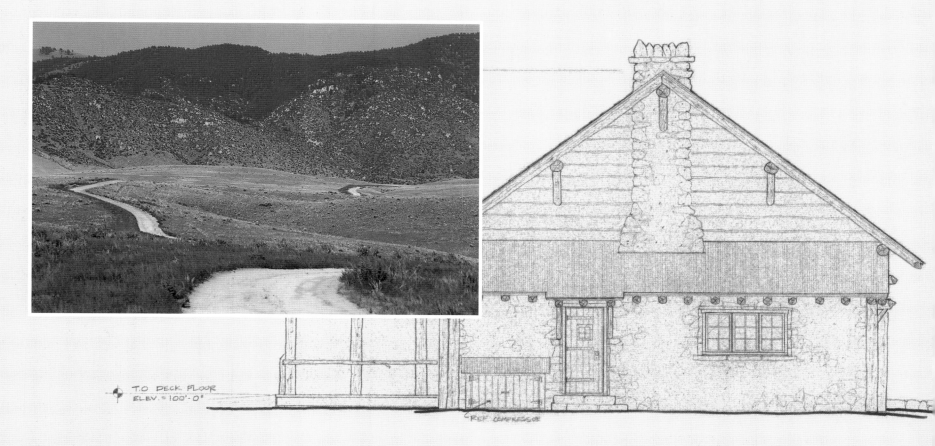

T.O. DECK FLOOR
ELEV.=100'-0"

REF. COMPRESSOR

NORTH ELEVATION
SCALE 1/4" = 1'-0"

O v e r l e a f :

(Left) Old timbers were cut and
used as siding on the camp
bunkhouses.

(Right) The road to the camp is
long and winding, and if you don't
know where you're going—you
just might get into trouble!

The drive up to the camp is along a dirt
trail, complete with rattlesnakes and rusted
cars. I'm certain that a creative art director
placed the autos to increase the ambiance
and mystique of the camp setting.

O p p o s i t e :

A magnificent fireplace in the dining hall is the perfect place for story-
telling on stormy nights.

RIVING ALONG the Big Hole River in
Montana can be an isolating experience. A turnoff comes and
I follow directions written on a scrap of paper. It's another long
road. Only one small restaurant with an open sign in the window is seen for miles. No cars or pick-ups are in the parking
lot. It's dry outside. An occasional coyote runs across the road.
I take another turn onto a lonelier road, and then a sharp left
turn over a tiny, one-lane bridge. I pass through an ancient
timber gate, onto a dirt road that I'm certain leads to nowhere.
I'm lost—I know it! The map from the car rental office shows
there are no roads here. I continue slowly, but still, nothing.

Eventually, gullies appear. One gully contains several
abandoned cars that are rusting away. I'm certain that rattlesnakes found them to their liking, so I don't explore the
vehicles—forget it! I drive on at ten miles an hour. Just dust
and high-desert plateaus are in view—no buildings, no signs,
no convenience stores. I drive farther and fully expect to see
cowboys and a stagecoach pulled by horses on the horizon. I'm
certain that Boot Hill is just around the next bend.

Half an hour later, I got my first glimpse of Two Moose
Camp. A Christian youth camp, the facility was conceived
years earlier by an individual who felt the need to do something that might improve the lives of urban youth.
Swimming, horseback riding, field games, great food, open

The backside of the main dining hall at the camp was made of local stones. This end of the hall houses the kitchen.

spaces—it's all there. Kids pay nothing to attend.

Yellowstone Traditions was approached and asked to get involved with the development of the camp. Each meeting between the property owners and the YT staff was preceded with a group prayer. The land itself, as described by Harry Howard of YT, was nothing less than "raw, uninhabitable and arid." Nonetheless, it did have great access to the Big Hole River. Harry was responsible for selecting the sight for the placement of the buildings. YT Studios acted as the architecture firm. In reality, only a few drawings were ever completed. YT was given total freedom to complete the job.

The meeting hall/dining facility resembles many of the old barns that inhabit the region. The building was stick-built and covered on both the interior and exterior with half-round, dead standing logs acquired from nearby forests. The roof was covered with shingles. The roof over the gabled entryway was covered with steel to facilitate snowmelt and slide-off. An extensive kitchen was constructed off the back end of the building and covered with vertical half-round logs. The west side of the building was completed with massive windows that allow for stunning views of the setting sun and the Big Hole River.

A stone addition that serves as a game room was completed off the south end of the building. The massive stone fireplaces and the stone game room were constructed by masonry wizard Rod Cranford of Bozeman, Montana. Campers eat at

The covered entrance to the hall has a dinner bell that can be heard from miles away.

In the summertime, the
grass and surrounding
cottonwood trees display
a brilliant green.

communal tables made of rough-cut pine boards. Mounted
game heads and antler chandeliers grace the hall.

A few hundred yards off the dining hall is a screen-
covered, open-air structure created from logs with a shingle
roof. The structure houses an assemblage of game tables and
protects the campers from nasty flying insects of all sorts. It's
also a shelter from the rain.

Down below are four traditional camp bunk cabins that
house kids and staff. A common shower house has barn-board
stalls and communal slate sinks. In front of the bunkhouses lie
three huge man-made ponds that serve as swimming holes for

The hall contains two massive fireplaces. Hickory chairs along with wooden benches provide seating for the campers.

Campers eat in the dining room on sawbuck tables made on-site. The ceiling fixtures were designed by Claudia Lee Foster.

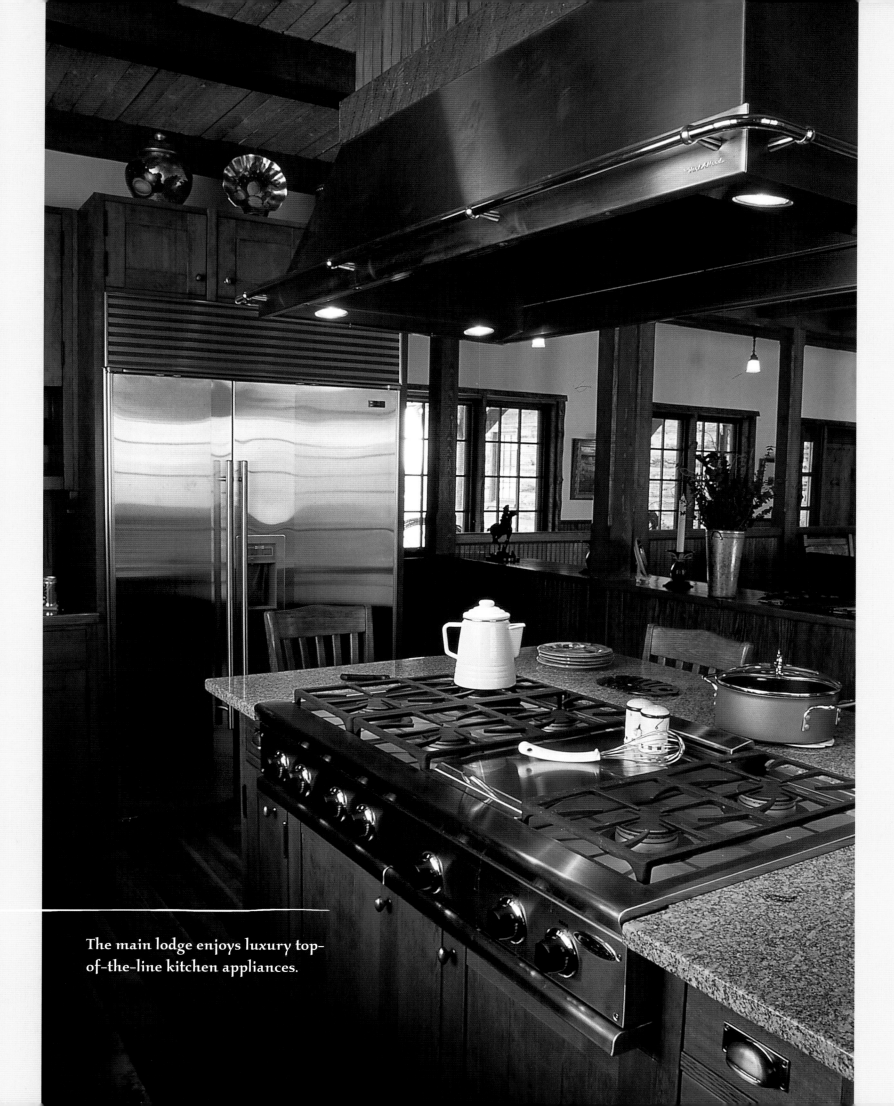

The main lodge enjoys luxury top-
of-the-line kitchen appliances.

Detail of the lodge roof levels at Two Moose Camp.

The structure shows weathered colors that blend perfectly with the surrounding hues.

the campers. The entire setting is relaxing, unpretentious and a tribute to owners, designers and contractors. If the camp weren't for kids only, I would certainly apply to attend.

A few hundred yards down the goat trail is the family lodge. Overlooking the Big Hole River, the compound is used frequently by the owners as a retreat from the world. The home was conventionally stick-built and covered with half-round logs on the interior and exterior. Justin Bowland was the superintendent for the 3,000-square-foot, four-bedroom home plus kitchen, dining room and living area. The bedrooms were completed with custom-made standard and bunk beds made from local antique barn boards. The beds, as well as the dining room table and chairs, were crafted at Yellowstone Traditions specifically for this project. The kitchen is complete with industrial-strength appliances.

The house remains a comfortable and sensible dwelling. Interior designer Claudia Lee Foster of Bozeman, Montana, styled the home with regional and contemporary art and furnishings. A grand piano in the family room overlooking the magnificent Big Hole River is played often by the owner. A massive fireplace crackles with the warmth of burning wood. The grand dining room table provides a common ground for family meals. The entire setting reverberates with history. Undoubtedly the ghosts of cowboys past roam the nearby foothills and look on the ranch, pleased and placated that the setting is there to not only increase the quality of life for the owners, but also for the hundreds of campers who pass through the gates each year. The world is a better place because of Two Moose Ranch.

The bathhouse for the camp boasts a tin roof and siding, combined with old pine boards. Like the old rusted autos on the long drive into the camp, the bath and other buildings look like they've been there for generations.

The stalls in the bathhouse were also made of old barn boards. Because of the dryness of the region, moisture does not stay around long enough to damage the materials.

93

The lodge living room offers leather seating and a grand piano to relax by. It is warmed during the day by sunlight from the wraparound windows and at night by a roaring fire. Old barn boards were used as flooring throughout the home.

A secluded spot in the living room invites relaxation and enjoyment of the sunset.

A granite top on the
counter allows for
ease in cleaning.

An open-air game room
has table games of all
sorts. (Below) The house
is used on rainy days and
to keep the bugs out.

The backside of the hall is cased with tall windows, allowing for dramatic views of the mountains and sunsets.

Opposite:

The dining room table and chairs were created in the YT workshop. The ten-foot tabletop is antique pine board.

Fir Creek Ranch

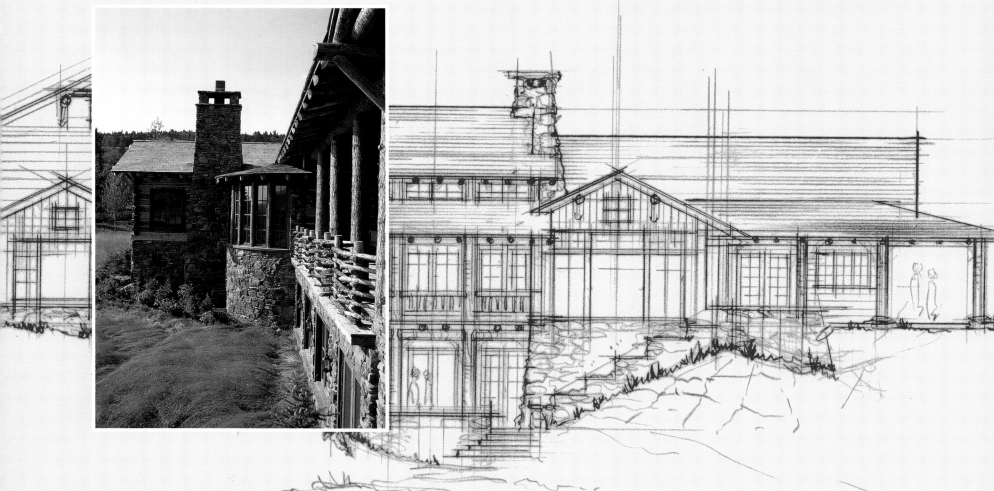

Overleaf:

Appearing as if the pile of boulders had always been there, a walkway traverses through the setting and leads to the lower level of the home. The full-notched construction is consistent with the historical homes in the area.

*D*RIVING NORTH from Jackson, Wyoming, one is immediately inspired by the sheer magnitude and richness of the environment. The Grand Tetons are the subject of Ansel Adams photographs, the Snake River is certainly one of the greatest-known fly-fishing meccas in the world, and an elk refuge hosting several thousand animals can send shivers down your spine. Known for its grand interpretation and presentation of architecture, the Jackson Hole setting inspires boldness, creativity and individuality.

For these discriminating clients, architect Larry Pearson, designer Diana Beattie, and the contractors/builders at Yellowstone Traditions sought to create a home inspired by the national parks and national heritage of the region. The site was once owned by the Rockefeller family and was designated as conservation easement land. Based on historical precedents, a home with hand-hewn logs and dovetailed construction was determined to be ideal for the setting.

Several restrictions were forced on the project by local and regional zoning commissions, regulating agencies and other enforcement bodies. The overall success of the project is attributed to Beattie and all involved for their uncompromising disposition of the integrity of the design and concern for the environment.

Blending per-
fectly with the
environment, the
ranch is a model
of both design
and comfort.

Opposite:

A side view of the home shows knee braces supporting a balcony off one of the many bedrooms.

Above:

Lindsey Kylloe relaxes on an antique hickory porch swing.

The entrance to the home is symmetrically well balanced. The wet footprints of the family dog, as seen on the sidewalk, lead directly into the home.

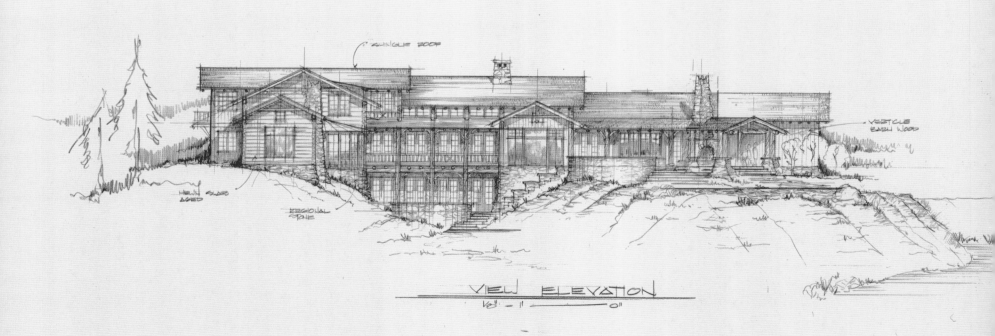

VIEW ELEVATION

A view of the front of the home through a "jack" fence suggests historical antecedents to the setting. In-ground sprinklers allow the vegetation to flourish.

An interior view of one of the many rooms in the home shows comfortable upholstered living room chairs, a rustic coffee table and paintings. The chandelier was made from the antlers of fallow deer.

The home is a continuum of experiences. One room leads to another, whose function is different from the next.

Of utmost importance was that the house blend with the environment and, second, that it appear as if it had always been there. Pearson sited the home on a ridge that provided and initiated a highly dramatic sequence of views. Consequently, the vital energy of the home unveils itself in both the immediate environment and in the dramatic scenery. To the west, the majestic Grand Tetons and the free-form Buffalo River offer unsurpassed and ever-changing vistas of the countryside. To the east, the views include a vista of the prairie and a cattle ranch.

The clients' utmost request was that it become a family home. The wife was also clear in that she wanted sufficient natural light so that it didn't become dark in the hallways and inside rooms, as large cabins are prone to do. She wanted flowing lines and roundness incorporated in both the interior and exterior of the home rather than squares or continuous straight lines. To meet her needs, a round turret was designed for the building.

The owners preferred flat, stacked stones as opposed to the river rock indigenous to the region and found on the property. Eagle sandstones brought in from Montana were horizontally stacked according to the designs of the architect. The intricate stonework for the fireplaces, foundations and patios was completed by Ron Cranford.

The setting allowed for a full basement that houses entertainment rooms and two offices. All together, the house includes five bedrooms, two offices, eight baths, a sauna, game room, kitchen, living room, and numerous fireplaces. The house was conventionally framed and the notched logs were applied to the exterior of the building. A sawmill was created

Painted by Jennifer Besson, the yellow walls add life to the setting. The soft blue colors on the upholstered furniture complement the earth tones of the structure. (Right) Oversized, upholstered club chairs occupy a delicate corner in the circular turret of the home.

Numerous fireplaces throughout the home allow family members and guests a bit of private time.

The interior of the building includes numerous built-in bookcases, desks and other creations. Interior designer Diana Beattie has been credited with the completion and success of the project.

The family dining room includes upholstered hickory chairs. The floor of the home was created from rough-cut pine boards.

on the property to prepare the seasoned, antique timbers that went into the building. All notching and dovetailing was completed on-site. In addition, a fire-retardant system was installed. The structure is heated with radiant heat.

Stump-based, bark-on western red cedar trees were used as columns for the many porches. Traditional jack-leg fencing was incorporated into the outdoor setting to restrict the movement of the horses and cows.

Of further importance to the home's appeal is the landscaping. Sheep fescue grass was planted to give it a pioneer flavor. An in-ground sprinkler system provides needed moisture and keeps the grass green.

Diana Beattie engaged artist Jennifer Besson to paint the walls and to insure that the colors in the home were both light and lively. The owners' kids chose their own colors for their rooms.

The entire setting is a sensation of comfort. The evenings are often spent gazing at the Tetons scenery or fly-fishing in the Beaver River just a stone's throw from the house. Horses come around, wanting to be fed and scratched. And an occasional newborn calf inspires wonderment.

The built-in desk and bookshelves were constructed from rough-cut pine boards. The chairs are from the Old Hickory Furniture Company in Indiana.

This bathroom vanity was covered with cherry and willow shoots.

Another bath contains this copper bowl and faucets. The walls were wallpapered with old, historical Wyoming maps.

Old barn boards were used to construct this vanity. The bowl and faucets are made of copper.

Opposite:

A downstairs recreation room includes a pool table, game table and a warming fireplace.

Opposite:

Bark-on western red cedar
was used for the pillars
throughout the structure.
Along with adding charac-
ter to any building, a profound sense of humor is
inherent in naturally
formed logs.

Traversing the backside of
the home, the chimney
lines fit perfectly with the
architectural lines of the
pillars and columns.

A winding staircase leads
to the patio and stunning
views of the Grand
Tetons.

The Hacienda

Overleaf:

The wet sink in the kitchen has a copper bowl and designer faucet. The hearth over the stove demonstrates organic design.

The main entrance is secured by a handmade double door edged with hand-hammered metal moldings.

*T*HE COLORS THAT SURROUND YOU are the soft colors of sand. The brightest of the hues are the subtle rust reds that glow from the rocks. Small, foreboding plants, heavily adorned with sharp points, thorns and stickers discourage visitors. Tall saguaro cacti stand like sentinels guarding the land. An occasional javelina pig runs across the road. Many of the winding roads are unmarked. It is very dry. One immediately wonders why in heaven early immigrants would settle in this land. That plants and animals evolved here is a testament to the persistence and power of life itself.

From the private drive it is impossible to either see or comprehend the complete setting that lies before you. Blending perfectly with the environment and hidden by immaculate indigenous landscaping, the home offers a profound historical interpretation of the classic Southwest Mission setting.

Architect Larry Pearson was originally brought in to "comment" on construction, placement and other concerns the owners had in regards to the initial drawings for their home. After considerable discussion, Larry was hired to revamp and completely redesign the plans. In time the project evolved in the Mission style,

Opposite:

An in-ground pool just off the side porch allows the owners a refreshing moment before they have dinner on the patio.

SOUTH ELEVATION
1/8" = 1' - 0"

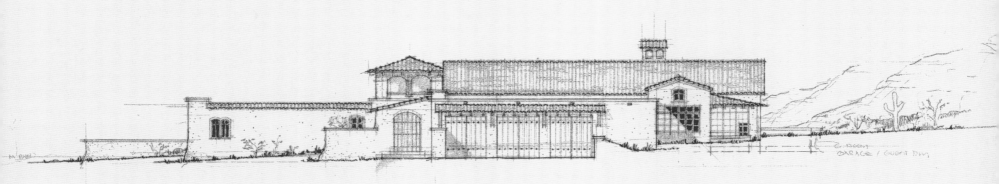

EAST ELEVATION
1/8" = 1' - 0"

based on historical precedents of the Southwest territory. The setting is isolated, like a monastery.

Set on an axis that allows for visions of both the rising and setting sun, the home offers stunning views of the mountainous national-forest backdrop and the urban valley below. Ultimately, Pearson conceived and designed a home that flowed with continuous, integrated experiences centralized around a sensuous nave that includes a traditional circular fountain.

The home itself is more of an experience than a structure. Wanting it to blend with the environment, the owners encouraged and supported significant landscaping. Although made of stones and minerals, the home speaks of organic nature. Sunlight dances through the compound, illuminating the subtle nuances. Sometimes direct and sometimes subdued, the effects of sunlight proffer an ever-changing vision of the dwelling.

Known for their desire and ability to instill creativity in those who work for them, the homeowners both encouraged and empowered everyone associated with the project to offer solutions and suggestions concerning the construction of the home. They wanted something authentic. They did not seek a Hollywood reenactment of Mission style. They wanted the real thing. The results of this effort are obvious.

The construction wizards at Yellowstone Traditions oversaw the project. They were encouraged to utilize their unique abilities to complete a high-tech home within the realm of classic Spanish Colonial architecture. Todd Gardener from YT constructed many of the pieces of furniture that

A section of the home reveals creative masonry and classic southwestern architecture.

occupy the home. Not only the owners but their design mentors, Ed Holler and Sam Saunders, scoured South American and the warehouses of Old Mexico for original colonial Spanish furnishings and architectural inspiration from the seventeenth century. The pictures were acquired from Ed Holler and Sam Saunders, Ltd., of Nogales, Arizona. At the same time local, native artists were brought in to construct the home and insure its authenticity. Blacksmiths and craftsmen from Mexico to Montana

A pool table occupies a section of the living room and is complemented by historical furnishings.

Opposite:

Artists working within the realm of Spanish Colonial furnishings consistently demonstrate the use of unusual materials and originality.

A dramatic interior door shows how the use of old materials can enhance a setting. Designed specifically for the home, this door and many others within the home clearly indicate quality and artistic endeavor.

Opposite:

This highly luxurious writing desk was created in the design studios of Yellowstone Traditions. A built-in book case houses a few of the owner's many books.

constructed all the hardware, windows and other necessities for the home.

Upon entering the compound, one is immediately overcome by the warmth of the home. The gentle curves and transitional angles within the dwelling render immediate comfort to the setting. The soft light that emanates through the windows and doorways is nothing less than relaxing. Courtyards allow for the viewing of dramatic sunsets. Further, the old-world appeal of the project is profound. In a positive sense, the place looks old, feels old and sounds old. Even the tile roof has an authenticity: each tile was made by bending pliable clay over a knee and then firing it in a kiln to maintain its correct symmetry.

The interior design of the building is monastic. The

The soft, organic lines, center fountain
and built-in bookcases are part of the
nave. Built as the center of the home, the
nave serves as the demarcation point for
the various rooms in the structure.

One of several bathrooms in the home, this facility offers in-floor radiant heat and built-in vanities. The high transom windows allow the room a soft reflection. The chandelier is of classic colonial design.

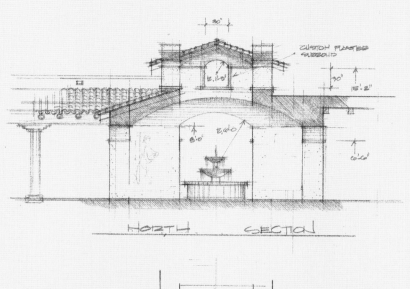

NORTH SECTION

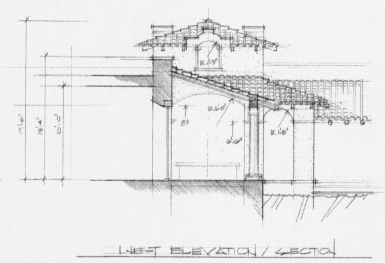

WEST ELEVATION / SECTION

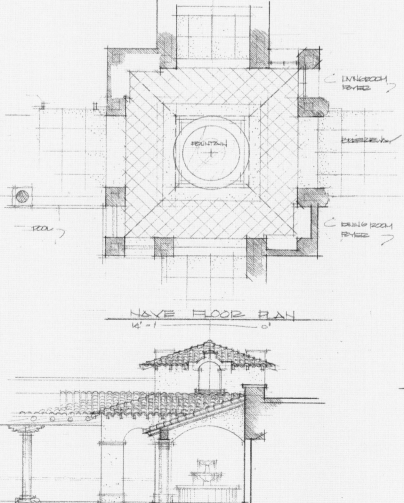

NAVE FLOOR PLAN

SOUTH ELEVATION / SECTION

A quiet corner in the dining room offers the owners a place to read and watch the sun set.

A classic Spanish Colonial dining set is enhanced by ornate candlesticks and serving bowls.

O p p o s i t e :

A pair of classic armchairs and an accompanying lamp table occupy a prominent place in the dining room. Spanish Colonial corbels brace the inlaid ceiling beams.

setting is purposefully left uncluttered. Soft, natural light illuminates and gives definition to individual objects of art. An occasional hidden spotlight adds further subtle distinction. The colors of the walls reflect the colors inherent in the immediate landscape and blend perfectly with many of the furnishings throughout the house.

The finished statement of the home is personal in nature. It is a place to relax and celebrate a historical style brought about through the inspiration and efforts of those who came before. And this place that will long be remembered after we are gone.

A highly ornate, seventeenth-century, gold-gilded corner cupboard rests in the dining room.

A further view of the dining room shows the ancient barn boards that were used for both the floor and ceiling.

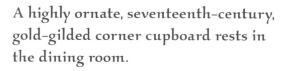

The main dining room contains a massive pine table surrounded by a set of tall-backed leather-upholstered dining chairs. A variety of antique items, including chandeliers, candlesticks and serving bowls, complement the setting.

The kitchen at the Hacienda was designed in classic southwestern style. Recessed drawers, ornate columns , moldings and knee braces, bold lines and intricate tiles make up the kitchen area.

A further view of the kitchen reveals the elaborate design of the center island, which houses two built-in dishwashers and wet sinks. Bricks were vertically inlaid in the floor to create an intricate, eye-dazzling pattern.

Another angle of the kitchen depicts the hidden, built-in
refrigerators. The sunlight from the skylight bathes the room
with a warm glow.

A further view of the
kitchen shows the char-
acter of the ceiling and
how it's enhanced by the
use of antique timbers.

O p p o s i t e :

The master bedroom
contains this four-
poster king-size pine-
apple bed. A floor-to-
ceiling door allows the
owners quick exit to the
outside gardens.

Landscapes designed by Arnold Rascon insure that something is always blooming. Bougainvilleas, petunias, yucca plants and numerous types of vegetation greatly enhance the setting.

Opposite:

A small trail exhibits intricate brickwork and beautiful landscaping.

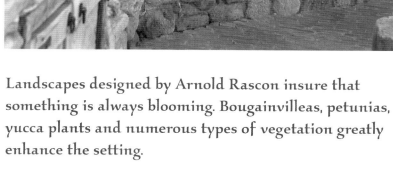

Though appear-
ing old, the
gates and many
other creations
within the com-
pound are actu-
ally new. Built
of old materials,
such embellish-
ments take on
significant
character.

The materials for the gate were standing-dead logs found in the area. Gates are kept closed at all times to prevent wild pigs from entering the grounds and consuming the succulent vegetation!

Giant saguaro cacti stand as sentinels in the desert setting. Wildlife of all sorts, such as deer, bobcats, and mountain lions, wander the nearby hills and mountains and are frequent visitors to the Hacienda.

147

A fireplace enhances a corner of the yard where a stone dining set is often the site of afternoon lunches and evening cocktails. (Right) A small, shallow pool ends abruptly at the foot of one of many fire pits on the property

The traditional terra-cotta roof tiles were individually handmade. The contours for the tiles are created by bending pliable clay over one's knee and then firing the clay in a kiln.

Opposite:

Many a happy day is spent on the patio of the Hacienda. Diners are often served poolside on this traditional Spanish Colonial dining set.

West Fork Camp

Hidden in the northern Rockies is West Fork Camp. The drive to it requires constant attention and nerves of steel. Reminiscent of a forest service camp, the compound is privately owned.

A period Arts and Crafts lamp sits on an early round table by the Old Hickory Furniture Company of Martinsville, Indiana.

WANDERING DOWN a winding mountain road high in the northern Rockies, I marvel at incredible vistas and rugged terrain. I am careful not to drive too close to the edge of the road, as one slight mistake could easily initiate a thousand-foot drop onto jagged rocks below. One quickly learns to pay attention to the driving here and to not linger too long on the joys of the vistas.

I turn left onto a path that brings new meaning to the term *road*. I'm surprised that the tires haven't blown out, as the edges of sharp rocks seem destined to meet with the rims of the wheels. I drive slowly for several minutes, avoiding the marmots and picas that scramble in front of me. A small, towerlike building reveals itself up ahead. I don't really know what it is. I approach slowly and another small cabin appears. I feel like I've been transported a hundred years back in time.

Owned by an international sports legend and his family, this complex of four small rustic homes was designed by Larry Pearson. Seeking a cluster of small cabins that would surround a centrally located

Blending into the immediate environment, this cabin is complete with office, bedroom, baths, kitchens and fireplaces.

Looking like its been there since the turn of the past century, this cabin in the West Fork Camp compound was constructed with rocks and timbers located on the property.

family lodge, the homes were individually designed to reflect the personalities of the owners. Pearson and the contractors describe the clients as sophisticated and astute in taste, with passionate appreciation for the finer things in life. Pearson characterizes them as the perfect clients, sincere and respectful in every way. The casual, easy approach of the clients allowed him significant freedom in his approach to both designing and developing the compound.

The property, located in a vast, northern Rocky Mountain gated community, was initially suggested by Harry Howard of Yellowstone Traditions, whose company constructed the complex. Once the property had been selected, the builders and architect spent significant time snowshoeing and skiing the terrain to identify the correct site for each building.

There is a profound sense of folk art within the setting. The architects and builders continually describe the process as being completed with a sense of humor and sophistication.

During my five-week stay at the complex, I was thrilled by the overall comfort and uniqueness of the entire setting. In the early morning, herds of elk wandered past my front door. A moose occasionally roamed within site, and daily I

A detail photo of the living room in the upper house depicts historical furnishings, as well as a custom-made entertainment center that houses a large-screen TV and other electronics.

Opposite:

An assemblage of antique Arts and Crafts furniture in the upper cabin blends perfectly with the geometric lines inherent with log cabins.

spent time with the dozens of friendly marmots that inhabited a rock outcropping on the property. Birds of prey soared through the skies and an occasional bear wandered nearby. Nonetheless, the sunsets were the most inspirational part of the day. I marveled at the dramatic changes each evening in the vast skies and landscape views. As a further bonus, two well-stocked trout ponds kept me busy and world-class fly-fishing was located within ten minutes of the

This bathroom sink sits on a cabinet covered with half-round pine logs.

Framed by timbers and burls, the kitchen, though open to the dining room, seems entirely separated.

complex. It was difficult for me to leave when the time came.

Once through the guarded gatehouse, the road traverses through alpine mountains and descends to an unmarked dirt road that leads to the property. The owner, who had long been fascinated with "parkitecture," suggested that Pearson model one structure on the fire towers built by the National Park Service in the early parts of the past century. In this building he not only wanted to be able to spend time with his family

but also enjoy a Scotch and a cigar with his buddies while overlooking the vast terrain. Further, he wanted the absolute authenticity of a Forest Service camp.

The result is perhaps one of the most dramatic residential settings ever. Small in scale, the firehouse towers over the landscape. With period Arts and Crafts furnishings, the setting is a model of comfort. Downstairs, a bedroom and bath offer private quarters. The house also offers a second-floor kitchen, bath and built-in bunk beds. The top floor includes built-in bench seating, period rockers and an exterior walkway with views that can mesmerize even the most experienced sightseers.

Built mostly of flat-stacked stones, the home also includes extensive log work. Cut from dead standing timber, the logs were artistically scribed and darkened to appear as if the entire building had been there for generations.

A view of the kitchen in the upper house shows an advanced design, including a copper vent over the stove, slate-covered counters and burls.

Made in the 1930s in the Jackson Hole area, this elk-antler arm-chair blends perfectly with the hues of the logs and stones.

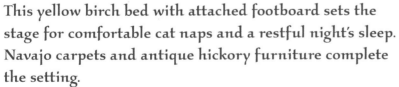

This yellow birch bed with attached footboard sets the stage for comfortable cat naps and a restful night's sleep. Navajo carpets and antique hickory furniture complete the setting.

An early antique twig rocker sits in the corner of the bathroom. Made of willow shoots and oak, such rockers are known for their unique designs and comfort.

A claw-foot tub with fancy hard-ware is heavenly for soaking tired muscles and weary bones.

Perfect symmetry of
lines adds to the
uniqueness and appeal
of this guest cabin.

Numerous hickory
rockers dress the back
porch of the guest cabin
at the West Fork Camp.

Symmetrical, geometric lines are also prominent in both Arts and Crafts style and prairie school designs.

The weathered door blends perfectly with the stones and notched, tongue-and-grove construction of the guest cabin.

The other buildings on the complex are unique in their own right. Seeking absolute simplicity, the owners wanted a compound that completely blended with the environment. They sought historical structures with low rooflines and organic materials that merged with the landscape. Constructed of local stone and timber, each retains its own personality. Consistent with the spirit of the Old West, the homes are marvels of engineering and design.

One of the cabins was constructed with full-scribed logs. The other log home was stick-built and split logs were applied to the interior and exterior of the building. Great pains were taken with all the

Opposite :

An early Gustav Stickley sideboard houses a collection of collectibles. A painting of Chief Joseph overlooks the gathering room.

A further view of the room depicts a blend of historical furniture, paintings and bronzes.

buildings to insure their sense of historical correctness as well as comfort. All the buildings are complete with period-looking modern conveniences, including electronics of all kinds, as well as comfortable and usable kitchens and bathrooms.

Neil Greathouse served as superintendent during construction. Ed Matos of Bridger Engineering took on the difficult task of engineering the project. The stonework was completed by Phil Cox and Logan Mize. The result is an ultimate statement of comfort and quality within the realm of rustic design.

Along with numerous Arts and Crafts pieces, the guest house also includes many pieces of original furniture by Thomas Molesworth.

Opposite:

The interior of this guest cabin offers a look at life in the west as it was being settled. Western furniture, paintings of landscapes and trout, and Arts and Crafts furniture are ideal for the setting.

The kitchen in the guest house offers stylish appliances, an Arts and Crafts dining set and a painted antique cupboard.

O p p o s i t e :

This bedroom in the guest house was constructed to look like an add-on, much as a settler's cabin would have received additions over the years.

Bunk beds in the guest house are adorned with "cushy" mattresses and colorful Navajo carpets. Recessed lighting in the ceiling offers a warm glow to the room.

169

The very fine workmanship of various craftsmen are visible in these chinked-log walls, hand-built window frames, and dry-stacked stone wall.

A massive chair adorned with moose and deer antlers sits on the porch of the trapper's cabin. The seat was made from a local pine tree. The front porch of the trapper's cabin is home to this mint-condition glider by the Old Hickory Furniture Company.

Two views of the trapper's cabin profile a low roofline and intricate stonework on the chimney. New "old" buildings on the property suggest historical structures. The pond is well stocked with aggressive trout!

Opposite:

A small rustic dining set made of pine seems perfect for the trapper's cabin.

The living room of the trapper's
cabin has space-saving built-in beds,
the bases of which are covered with
birch bark. Antique Arts and Crafts
rockers are perfectly at home.

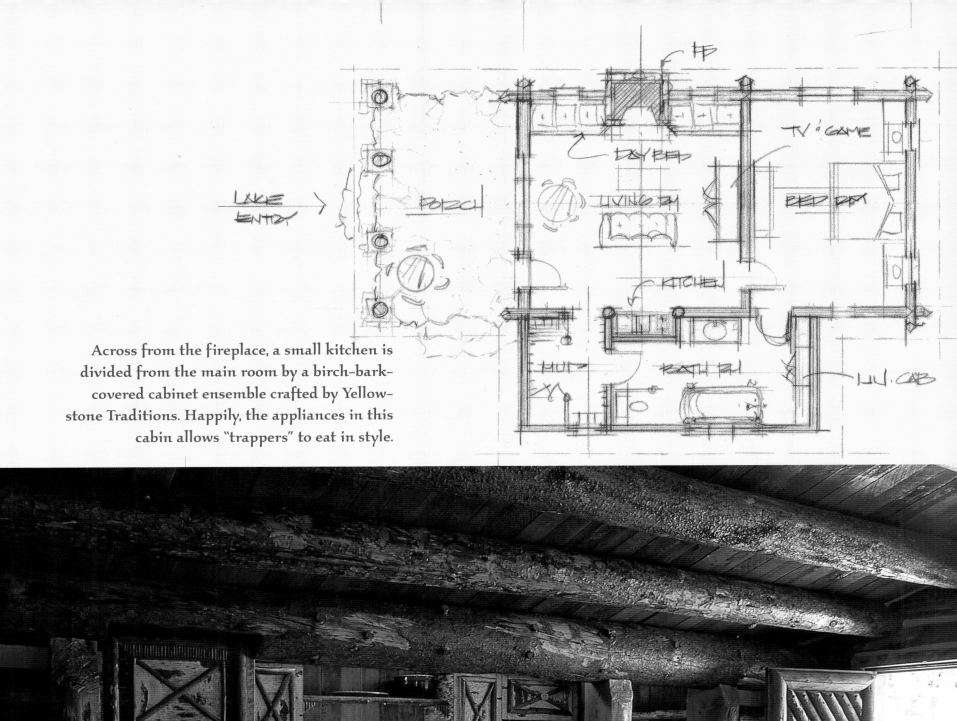

Across from the fireplace, a small kitchen is divided from the main room by a birch-bark-covered cabinet ensemble crafted by Yellow-stone Traditions. Happily, the appliances in this cabin allows "trappers" to eat in style.

Each custom door in the trapper's cabin was hand-built. and covered with half-round logs—further evidence of the attention to detail paid by Larry Pearson and the folks at YT.

At one end of the bathroom, a door provides entrance to a glorious shower and steam room.

Created with flat, stacked stones and ancient timbers, the fire tower is a work of art.

The balcony on the fire tower offers a
grand view of a private ski slope.

The master bedroom on the ground floor of the tower is outfitted with original Gustav Stickley furniture. Edward Curtis photographs adorn the walls.

The door into the down-stairs bedroom in the fire tower was custom made by YT. Heavy strap hinges add to the mys-tique and historical presence of the building.

The kitchen cabinets were built from rough-cut pine. A set of original Limberts table and chairs from the Arts and Crafts period add even more style.

Making the best use of limited space, the second floor of the fire tower includes three built-in bunk beds, a complete kitchen and a bathroom.

The top room in the fire tower is decorated with original Thomas Molesworth furniture and Navajo rugs. Benches are perfect for visiting or passing out on after a hard day of fishing or skiing.

Opposite:

The deck provides a bird's-eye-view of the compound and surrounding mountains. Marmots climbed the stairs and coaxed me into feeding them pounds and pounds of peanuts. A golf course is seen in the background.

Corral Creek Ranch

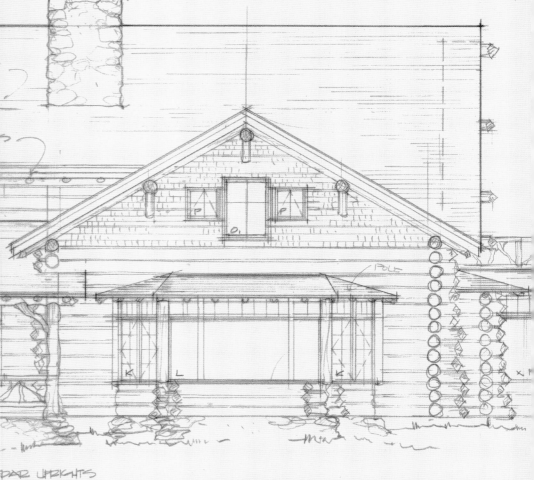

CEDAR UPRIGHTS
W/ ADIRONDACK STYLE
HANDRAIL DETAIL

ERHAPS THE GREATEST place on earth, the Corral Creek Ranch encompasses a little more than three thousand acres near the Madison River in southern Montana. Rolling hills that cascade down from towering peaks and wandering prairies make up the ranch. Wildlife is everywhere. A herd of nearly three thousand elk winter on the ranch. Eagles and osprey fish the ponds, badgers chase cars, deer wander throughout the family compound, and moose, bears and cougars have been known to frequent the estate.

Having accepted an invitation to spend some time at the ranch, I arrived at the lengthy driveway with my wife and three-year-old daughter on an early Monday morning. The drive up to the main buildings was made far more interesting by a herd of pronghorn antelope that raced alongside the car. I toyed with the thought, for just a moment, that the caretakers of the ranch released the antelopes from pens to create a fantasy arrival experience for my visit.

When we arrived at the gate I had to get out of the car and shoo away horses before I could open the fence to the compound. Once inside the enclosure, we were somewhat awestruck by the buildings and grounds, which appeared to have been there a hundred years although the buildings were of new construction; they blended perfectly with the environment.

A detail section of custom door blends perfectly with the ancient logs that were used on the house. Custom-made strap hinges and other hardware are visible throughout the house. The door was constructed antique timbers found locally.

Overleaf:

Fresh-cut flowers grace a western-influenced console table. The leather-trimmed mirror was made by Chris Chapman.

The entrance to the ranch begins through a typical western archway. On my first visit, several wild antelope ran alongside my vehicle. The Madison Range in the background is inhabited by animals of every sort found in the region.

Initially Harry Howard of Yellowstone Traditions was invited to construct a "line cabin" for the setting. Harry and his family lived on the property during construction, and his children were home-schooled within the Corral Creek setting. Rather than build a stunning "trophy" structure, a small, old-appearing and environmentally friendly building was constructed. Antique lumber and logs from old, torn-down Rocky Mountain cabins were used as the primary building materials. These materials made a significant statement in terms of uniqueness, hand-made quality, comfort and art.

Stains and sealers were not used on the exterior of the house with the intent of allowing the buildings to weather to a natural color reminiscent of the historical buildings that permeate the region's national forests and surrounding areas. At

The main home on the property was built on the footprint of an original lodge that was constructed in the early 1900s with the Madison Range as backdrop. Lindsey Kylloe feeds one of the many horses that call the ranch home.

The mailbox for Corral Creek Ranch was made from a variety of recycled woods found on the property. Antelope and elk are often seen in the fields behind the mailbox.

the same time, much of the material was culled from the property. Stones were collected for fireplaces, and "character wood" was found for the staircase and walkway banisters. Consequently, the nature of the design began to evolve as it became apparent "lived-in" would be the pervasive approach to the entire project, which encompassed more than a decade of construction.

At the same time, a journey just outside the buildings is an artistic experience in itself. Professional gardener Dale Dombroski was asked to have something blooming at all times during the summer, when the owners are in residence. The result of his innovation, meticulous care and knowledge is nothing less than magical. In a region of dry colors, the ranch is a constant bath of green. In time the owners sought a complex that both mimicked and rivaled turn-of-the-century cattle ranches. This was the setting that both of the owners had fantasized since their youth.

Conceived of years earlier, the owners toured eighty-four different real estate properties before settling on the Corral Creek property. The estate is a working cattle ranch that averages around three hundred and fifty head annually. Along with cattle, about twenty horses and an ancient donkey often walk up to you, demanding attention and a scratch behind their ears. The complex also boasts a small, quiet stream that is

This section of the porch is made more livable with Old Hickory furniture and elk antlers.

Opposite:

A side view of the front section offers a further view of the artistry that went into the creation of the home. Meticulous in detailing, the owners empowered the builders to create improvisational solutions to design and decorating, and encouraged artistic expression within the creation of the ranch.

home to easily the greatest trout fishing in the lower forty-eight. They even have their own subspecies aptly named Corral Creek cutthroat trout. These fish are darker than traditional cutthroat—and they fight like crazy!

But equally important as the buildings and grounds is the humanity that permeates the complex. The live-in cook, master chef Luke Pucket and his wife, Angie; ranch foreman Don Clark; cattle and ranch managers Peggy and Mark Jasmann; gardener Dale Dombroski and a host of others are honorary family members. What is unusual about the setting is that each of the ranch associates has been empowered by the owners to make decisions concerning the ranch. Moreover, the owners believe in tapping into the creative spirits of not only the immediate "ranch hands," but they also empowered the architects, builders and designers of the facility to use their collective ideas to create the setting. Everyone—from the cabinet builders to the masons—was encouraged to find creative solutions to artistic endeavors within the ranch setting.

This section of the home is an outside view of the owners' study/office.

The ranch is made up of several buildings, including the three-bedroom main lodge with servants quarters; a two-bedroom guest house; game hall with exercise room; state-of-the-art electronic media room and a full wet bar; and a garage that houses an absolutely classic ranch "woody." The complex further includes a high-elevation, single-room, sod-roofed line

cabin (complete with outhouse) that is frequented by the owners when on horseback, a small fishing cabin, a gorgeous Arts and Crafts–style barn in traditional rustic mode, and an additional collection of buildings that house ranch associates. The place is stunning!

The main house, designed by architect wizard Larry Pearson, was created on the footprint of the pre-existing structure. The interior of the house, designed by Hilary Heminway, is a marvel of comfort and convenience. The owner incorporated numerous high-end pieces of rustic furniture made by Jimmy and

One of the many porches at Corral Creek is complete with antique furniture from the Old Hickory Furniture Company in Martinsville, Indiana. Blooming flowers are a constant at the ranch. Bark-on western red cedar was used as columns for the porches.

Opposite:

A view of the rustic nature of the stonework, logs and landscaping that encompass the Corral Creek Ranch.

NORTH ELEVATION

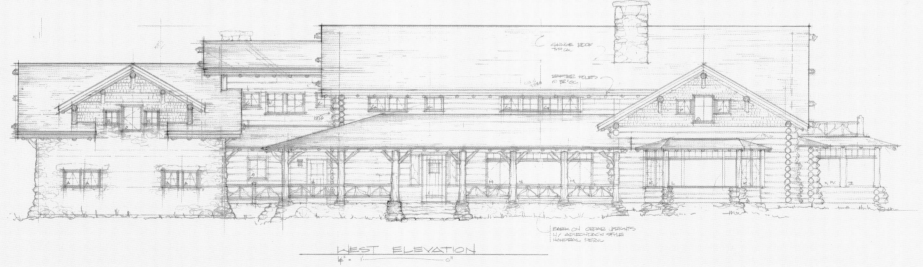

WEST ELEVATION

Visitors to the home are greeted by this dramatic sideboard made by Jimmy Covert. The western-motif oil painting reminds one that the wilderness is just outside the door.

O p p o s i t e :

Staircase leading to the second floor was made of lodgepole pine. The banisters were constructed with organic poles harvested in nearby forests. The floor to this entryway is covered with iron slate.

Linda Covert of Cody, Wyoming, and also included many pieces of traditional furniture, like those that would have been brought by pioneer families as they journeyed west.

Although the owners of the property consistently give credit to everyone except themselves, the wife has a degree in interior design and is consistently credited with innovative ideas and vision by almost everyone involved in the project. Built as a hands-on house, the facility frequently houses guests (like myself), family and friends. Additionally, the husband is a significant figure in the business world and has served as CEO and on numerous boards around the country. What makes him interesting is not only his perspective on the world, but also that during cattle round-ups he dons his cowboy outfit and rides his horse for the duration of the cattle drives.

With a full-time live-in chef, one might expect a certain

"attitude" from those affiliated with the ranch. Nothing could be farther from the truth. Rather, as an example of just the opposite, chef Luke Pucket goes on the cattle drives and cooks for the cowboys. It's the only cattle drive in America where the cowboys have tiramisu for dessert!

But what I found to be most refreshing is the attitude of the owners. They do not see themselves as the "owners" of the ranch, but instead view themselves as stewards of the property. They are only taking care of the extraordinary, artistic setting that they have both fostered and created.

An antique Black Forest hall tree is a receptacle for numerous hats. Made in Switzerland for the tourist trade, such bear hall trees are made of linden. The small, antique twig rocking chair was probably made in Pennsylvania or Ohio in the early 1900s.

O p p o s i t e :

Taxidermy, original western paintings, room-size Navajo carpets and related Indian artifacts greatly enhance the drama of the living room. The dry-stack masonry of the fireplace is an art.

Todd Gardiner of YT created the cupboard in classic antique style. Fresh-cut flowers are ever-present throughout the house.

An overview of the home indicates that log homes are decorated not only with rustic items but contemporary modern furnishings as well. An Arts and Crafts lamp and decorative pillows add to the setting.

This high-style armchair was made by Jimmy Covert. Linda Covert completed the chairs by covering them with decorative leather. Indian motifs decorate the lamp shade.

A floor-to-ceiling view of the living room offers the viewer a look at an integrated living space that accommodates a variety of styles of furnishings and décor.

In the dining room, the chairs surrounding the table were made by Lester Santos. A built-in cabinet houses dishes and glasses. An early cupboard made by Todd Gardiner of Yellowstone Traditions is made from locally cut lodgepole pine. The dimensional lumber is antique fir collected from torn-down structures in Montana.

The tall cupboard was created from recycled barn woods from the Rocky Mountains. The cabinet is complete with Arts and Crafts-influenced hardware. The top crest of the cabinet is adorned with a massive burl that adds a sense of ruggedness to the piece.

An oversized English side chair plays host to one of many antique Indian garments that grace the home.

The massive dining room table is surrounded by tall-back, leather-covered English dining chairs. The base for the table was created from massive stumps of fir trees. The table-top was made from four-inch-thick slabs of locally cut western fir trees. The shades on the table lamps are lined with pliable mica.

Opposite:

An interior view of the owners' study shows a leather-upholstered armchair and ottoman that invites relaxing moments of reading and leisure.

A floral-covered wing chair offers a place to rest and read in a secluded section of the home. The floor lamp was made from naturally shed elk antlers, which are often found on the property.

The interior of the house features reproduction Craftsman-style furnishings. The soft color theme throughout the home was developed by the owners.

The kitchen in the
main house is fin-
ished with a large
stainless steel indus-
trial stove.

The built-in cabinets
were made by Todd
Gardiner of YT.

Although the kitchen is small in size, the live-in master chef creates culinary adventures at each sitting. The bar stools were made by Todd Gardener.

This dramatic desk was made by rustic artist Jimmy Covert of Cody, Wyoming. The desk was masterfully made from walnut and locally harvested juniper. The metal inlay was created by Peter Fillerup. An antique Spanish-influenced chair rests against the wall.

A nook on the second-floor veranda of the main house includes this western-style armchair by Lester Santos of Cody, Wyoming.

Opposite:

Overview of the living room and entranceway. The Arts and Crafts lighting pieces were made by Michael Adams of Aurora Studios, New York.

A grand overview of
the living room at
Corral Creek Ranch.

Built-in shelves were added to house the owner's prodigious
collection of leather-bound books. Locally acquired antique pine
boards were used as flooring for many rooms in the house.

Built-in cabinets
throughout the house are
covered with half-round
logs made from stand-
ing-dead lodgepole pine
trees.

A four-poster bed made
of standing-dead lodge-
pole pine is a perfect
complement to the
rafters.

A large pine cupboard serves as a wardrobe in the corner of one of the many bedrooms. A continental armchair with burgundy upholstery occupies another corner. Todd Gardiner of YT.

A sectional view of one of many bathrooms in the home. Each door was designed and built by the folks at Yellowstone Traditions.

A small bedside
table was made
from half-
round, one-
inch-thick
lodgepole trees.

The master bedroom is complete with a four-poster bed, working fireplace, leather armchairs and related Navajo accessories.

Highly decorative leather pillows are used throughout the house as accent pieces.

Lindsey Kylloe plays with a toy goose while being guarded by the owners' trained attack dog!

Stone artistry is a theme at Corral Creek. Blooming flowers and meticulous landscaping add to a dramatic garden setting. Wrought-iron chairs host many happy conversations among ranch guests.

Organic western red cedar poles are used to support the many porches. Stones acquired from the property were used in flat-stack style throughout the home.

Opposite and above:

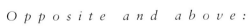

Detail of the back facade and extensive gardens. The stonework was completed by Phil Cox of Big Sky Masonry, Bozeman, Montana. The romance of the outside pathway is enhanced by rich ground coverings.

Complete with in-ground sprinkling system, the
grounds are consistently lush throughout the
changing seasons.

As requested by the owner, something must be blooming all the time at Corral Creek Ranch.

The back section of the
barn offers a drive-in
storage bin.

This magnificent barn, designed in the Arts and Crafts style, was drawn by Larry Pearson. Constructed with minimal tools, the project was made entirely with materials found on-site.

An extra-wide "designer" door in the barn allows easy access for the many horses that occupy the ranch.

The entertainment cabin, located a short walking distance
from the main house, is outfitted with a full bar. A pool table,
card table and entertainment room are for the guests' enjoyment. The entrance to the gaming hall is made highly dramatic
with careful attention to plants and greenery of all types. The
vestibule also serves as an outdoor barbecue and eating area.

The gaming hall offers this card table for wanna-be card sharks and gamblers. Made of hickory in Indiana, the chairs are covered with leather. The floors were made from rough-cut antique fir boards.

The in-house bartender at the gaming hall can keep track of funds with this antique cash register.

Visitors can wait for their turn at the pool table in this antique barber's chair! The antique bear stand will hold your pool cue while you use the spittoon!

The entertainment room in the gaming hall has oversized leather reclining chairs. The electronics were provided by Thirsty Ear in Bozeman, Montana. I personally sat up all night and watched all four episodes of *Star Wars*. It was a place to lose all contact with the world. I am certain that I was a Jedi knight in an earlier life!

A view of the front porch of the guest cabin. Master gardening artist Dale Dombroski sees to it that every aspect of the landscaping lives up to his exceptional expectations.

Overview of the guest cabin
at Corral Creek Ranch.

The large cabinet and beds in the
second-floor guest room of the
main house were made by New
West in Cody, Wyoming.

Rustic pillows and hides decorate the bed.

A corner in the guest house includes these two upholstered continental armchairs.

Perhaps nothing is more romantic or suggestive than a redone sheep wagon by designer Hilary Heminway. Functional in every way, many a happy hour have been spent relaxing around the fire and then retiring to the sounds of distant coyotes.

A full-size bed will bring comfort to any weary cowgirl worn out from a day on her Harley!

236

Among the wagon's antique kitchen gear are a cowboy coffee pot, wash pails, cups of all sorts and pan-cake flippers!

High above the main lodge, Harry Howard of Yellowstone Traditions built this line cabin. Accessible only on horseback, the materials for the cabin were cut on-site.

The dining room furniture includes this saw-buck table and benches. A wood stove takes the chill off cool nights.

238

The interior of the cabin contains built-in bunk beds, a dining area, an assortment of rustic collectibles and Navajo rugs.

239

Another view of the
line cabin interior.
Old barn boards were
used as dimensional
materials for the cab-
inets and drawers
beneath the beds.

Hickory chairs blend
perfectly with the
immediate environ-
ment of the line
cabin.

An organic gate leads to a corral and tack house that adjoin the high-elevation line cabin.

The two-hole outhouse was designed by Larry Pearson.

A few hundred yards from the main house rests this new (built to look old) fisherman's cottage. The cabin offers a grass-covered roof and rests next to the finest trout pond in Montana.

An antique Black
Forest bear holds a
tray full of fly-fishing
flies for guests.

A rustic bed in the
fisherman's cabin
allows a weary soul to
relax if the fish aren't
biting.

Opposite:

The interior of the fly-fishing
cabin includes a fireplace,
antique hickory furniture and
a variety of cabin collectibles.

Resources

ARCHITECTS

Larry Pearson
Architects, AIA
PO Box 3666
Bozeman, MT 59772
406.587.1997
866.587.1997
or
PO Box 2320
Bigfork, MT 59911
406.837.0201
877.235.2951
www.lpaia.com

Candace Tillotson-Miller
Architect, AIA
PO Box 470
Livingston, MT 59047
406.222.7057
fax: 406.222.7372
www.ctmarchitects.com

BUILDERS/CONTRACTORS

Yellowstone Traditions
PO Box 1933
Bozeman, MT 59771
406.587.0968

Elephant Builders
William Keshishian
PO Box 117
Gallatin Gateway, MT
59730
406.763.4648

On Site Management, Inc.
417 W. Mendenhall St
Bozeman, MT 59715
406.586.1500

INTERIOR DESIGNERS/DECORATORS

Diana Beattie Interiors
1136 Fifth Ave
New York, NY 10128
212.722.6226
or
Double-D Homestead
McAllister, MT 59740
406.682.5700

Montana Wagons
Hilary Heminway/
Terry Baird
PO Box 1
McLeod, MT 59052
406.932.4350 or
860.535.3110

Hilary Heminway,
Designer
140 Briarpatch Rd
Stonington, CT 06378
860.535.3110

Claudia Lee Foster
37 E. Main St, Ste 9
Bozeman, MT 59715
406.587.3234

FURNITURE BUILDERS

Montana Custom
Furniture Company
David Coffin
705 East Mendenhall
Bozeman, MT 59715
406.582.8980
www.mtfurniture.com

Lester Santos
2208 Public St
Cody, WY 82414
307.587.6543

Jimmy and Linda Covert
2007 Public St
Cody, WY 82414
307.527.5964

David Laitinen
PO Box 286
McAllister, MT 59740
406.580.2395

New West
2811 Big Horn Ave
Cody, WY 82414
307.587.2839
www.newwest.com

Doug Tedrow
PO 3446
Ketchum, ID 83340
208.726.1442

RUSTIC DESIGN/FURNITURE GALLERIES

Ralph Kylloe Gallery
PO Box 669
Lake George, NY 12845
518.696.4100

Historic Montana Homes
Resource Center
PO Box 161429
Big Sky, MT 59716
406.995.3600

Fighting Bear Antiques
PO Box 3790
375 South Cache Dr
Jackson, WY 83001
307.733.2669

Sagebrush Interiors and
Gallery
661 Sun Valley Rd
PO Box 10014
Ketchum, ID 83340
208.726.9662

American West Gallery
520 4th St
PO Box 3130
Ketchum, ID 83340
208.726.1333

HOME ELECTRONICS/ENTERTAINMENT CENTERS

Thirsty Ear HI-FI
9 East Main St
Bozeman, MT 59715
406.586.8578

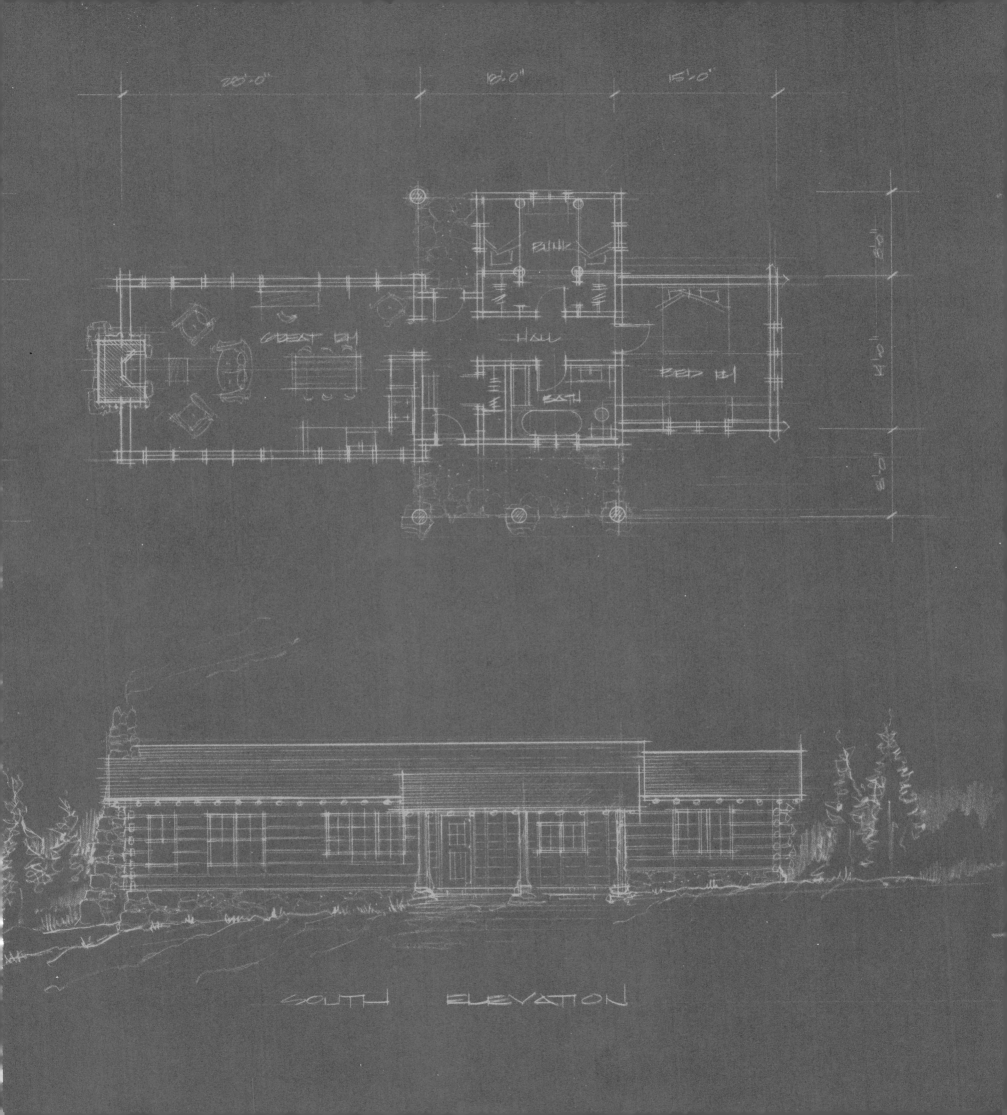

SOUTH ELEVATION

SOUTH – WEST   ELE

1/8" = 1'   0"